THE MEGA KIDS' JOKE BOOK

THE MEGA KIDS' JOKE BOOK

Hundreds and hundreds of useless,
corny, stupid, pointless jokes that you
will love to bits !

Collected and Illustrated by

PETER COUPE

For Lauren CR

Published by Arcturus Publishing Limited
For Index
Unit 1
Henson Way
Kettering
Northants
NN16 8PX

This edition published 1998

Printed and bound in Finland

© Peter Coupe / Arcturus Publishing Limited

ISBN 1 900032 62 7

Contents...

Nutty Names...

What do you call a man who writes
joke books for a living?

Poor!

What do you call a man with a cable
coming out of his ear ?

Mike !

What do you call a man who does
everything at top speed ?

Max !

What do you call a man who fills himself
with fried slices of potato and makes a
noise in the cinema ?

Chris Packet !

What do you call a super hero who
looks after books ?

Conan the Librarian !

What do you call an overweight vampire ?

Draculard !

What do you call a woman who works
for a solicitor ?

Sue !

What do you call a man who goes fishing
every weekend ?

Rod !

What do you call a
teacher with earplugs in ?

Anything you like - he
can't hear you !

What do you call a failed lion tamer ?

Claude Bottom !

What do you call twin brothers with drums on
their heads ?

Tom, Tom !

What do you call a man and woman who show you up in front of your friends ?

Mum and Dad !

What do you call a man who likes drawing and painting ?

Art !

What do you call a man who does odd jobs and lives just round the corner ?

Andy !

Prisoner - It's not my fault. I was given a name that was bound to lead me into crime !

Judge - *What is your name ?*

Prisoner - Robin Banks !

What do you call a woman who hates butter ?

Marge !

What do you call a 35 stone sumo wrestler ?

Whatever he tells you to !

What's the name of that really strict teacher

Miss Norder - Laura Norder !

What do you call a man who corrects examination papers ?

Mark !

What do you call a man with seagulls on his head ?

Cliff !

What do you call a woman who only comes out at Christmas ?

Carol !

What do you call a masked man who lends you money ?

The Loan Arranger !

What do you call a woman who checks punctuation ?

Dot !

I call him Bill - he's always asking me for money !

Did you hear about the man who used to make his living selling refreshments in the interval at football matches ?

His name.......... Alf Time !

What do you call a
Scotsman with his own
computer?

Mac!

★

What do you call a woman
who can makes pints
disappear in a pub?

Beatrix!

★

What do you call a man who keeps pet rabbits?

Warren!

★

What do you call a man who
keeps pet rabbits and
writes epic novels?

Warren Peace!

★

What do you call a man who
keeps an angry ferret down
his pants?

Very, very stupid!

What do you call the man who stamps the letters at the Post Office ?

Frank !

★

What do you call a man who works in a perfume shop at Christmas ?

Frank in Scents !

★

What do you call a woman having a meal in a restaurant ?

Anita !

★

What do you call a Spanish woman having a meal in a restaurant ?

Juanita !

★

If you really loved me, You'd let me call you Jack. Then you could lift my car and mend the puncture at the back !

What do you call a girl who has her own car ?

Minnie !

Is it true... that the man who invented the toilet was called...

...Lou ?

What do you call someone with more money than sense ?

My best Pal !

The dimmest boy in my class has the same initials as the contents of his head.....M.T.

⭐

What do you call a woman who has a boat tied up at the riverside ?

Maude !

What do you call a man with loads of money ?

Rich !

What do you call a fish that
tunes pianos ?

A Piano Tuna !

What do you call Mr Smith's half brother ?

Arthur Smith !

What do you call a
magician's assistant ?

Trixie !

What do you call someone
who never blows his nose ?

Ronnie !

What do you call a man who likes to grow flowers, fruit and vegetables ?

Gordon !

What do you call the brother and sister who like to build things across rivers ?

Archie and Bridget !

What do you call a girl who likes to cook in the garden ?

Barbie !

What do you call a woman with a food processor on her head ?

Belinda !

Who was the first man to do maths ?

Adam !

What do you call a man who hosts a quiz show
at Christmas ?

Santa Clues !

What do you call someone who claps when
contestants get the right answer ?

Santapplause !

What do you call the camel with three humps
that fell off the wall and smashed into millions
of pieces ?

Humphrey Dumpty !

★

What do you call
a man who lies in
front of your
door all day ?

Matt !

What do you call a girl with lots of suitcases ?

Carrie !

What do you call cattle thieves who wear tissue paper trousers ?

Rustlers !

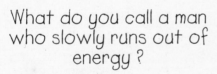

That frog is a secret agent - his name's Pond,

James Pond !

What do you call a man who slowly runs out of energy ?

Peter !

What do you call a girl who never stands up straight ?

Eileen !

What do you call
a girl who lives
in a pond ?

Lily !

★

What do you call
a nun with a
radio on her
head ?

A Transister !

★

What do you call
a teacher who
eats toffees in
class ?

A Chew-tor !

★

What do you call the man who carries a
football team from one match to another ?

The coach !

★

What do you call someone that witches go to when they are sick ?

A witch doctor, of course !

What do you call an Eskimo's house if it doesn't have a toilet ?

An Ig !

What do you call a house in France with two toilets ?

Toulouse !

What do you call it when a toilet is closed and bricked up ?

Loo - brick - ation !

What do you call the gap in a play for going to the toilet ?

The Interlude !

What do you call a teacher who has a
lot of accidents ?

Miss Hap !

What do you call the hairstyle you get from
sticking your head in an oven ?

A Micro - wave !

What was the name of the explorer with a
passion for biscuits ?

Captain Cookie !

What do you call the boy who is also a goat ?

Billy !

What do you call the woman who brings him to
school every day ?

His Nanny !

What do you call
someone who
gets paid to go to
college ?

Grant !

What do you call a cat
that eats lemons ?

A Sourpuss !

What do you call a
chicken that eats
cement ?

A Bricklayer !

What do you call the
ghost of a Star Trek
character ?

Doctor Spook !

What do you call a loud
mouthed soccer fan ?

A foot bawler !

What do you call a jogger
in a safari park ?

Fast food !

What do you call the
box a toad keeps
his tools in ?

A Toadstool box !

What do you call a
ghosts favourite
TV soap ?

Horror Nation Street !

What do you call a
executioners
favourite TV programme ?

Noose at ten !

What do you call a cricketer
who only
plays at night ?

The Star player !

What do you call the man
who serves fizzy drinks in your house ?

Pop !

What do you call 36 inches when you're in
Glasgow ?

A Scoland Yard !

What do you call the pudding that fought at the battle of the Little Big Horn ?

General Custard !

What do you call a parrot when he has dried off after a heavy rainstorm ?

Polly Unsaturated !

What do you call a man that people sit on in meetings ?

The Chairman !

What do you call a vicar on a Honda 750 motorbike ?

The Rev, rev, rev !

What do you call the place where spooks go for their holidays ?

A Ghost House !

What do you call a cake that is exactly the same as another cake ?

A Carbun copy !

I call him **Tod** - he keeps rabbits !

What do you call a miniature version of one of the Beatles ?

Small McCartney !

What do you call a pet that makes a lot of noise ?

A Trumpet !

What do you call a
computer's favourite
cake ingredient ?

Electric currents !

★

What do you call a
woman who
lets you
borrow money ?

G-Lenda !

★

What do you call a
man made up of
spare body parts ?

Hand Toe Knee !

★

What do you call a bear that plays
with Prince Charles ?

A Polo Bear !

What do you call a
ghost who picks
his nose ?

A Bogeyman !

What do you call
a young bee ?

A Baby !

What do you call a
bee with feathers ?

A Buzzard !

Which famous battle
did bees fight in ?

Battle of Hastings !

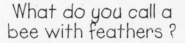

What do you call a bee with his own car ?

A Bee-M-W !

★

Is it true...

that the man who invented ice came from...

...Cuba ?

★

What do you call your brother's smelly son ?

My ne-phew !

★

What do you call an uncontrollable cat ?

Impussible !

What do you call a
woman who rescues
shipwrecked sailors ?

Mandy Lifeboats !

★

What do you call a
Scottish android ?

Robot the Bruce !

★

What do you call a man with three legs ?

Nothing - he's certain to catch you if you do !

★

What do you call the
steak and kidney
pudding that hit an
iceberg ?

The Pietanic !

What do you call
someone who talks to
his houseplants ?

Potty !

What do you call a
glass robot ?

See - Through - P - O !

A garage owner called his first daughter
Toyah, then he called his second daughter
Toyah as well...

She was the spare Toyah !

What do you call a
Roman emperor
who has
adventures ?

An action Nero !

What do you call the
detective who catches
underwear thieves ?

Nick. R. Lastic !

What do you call a
radio presenter who
plays records in
alphabetical order ?

An A, B, C, D, J !

What do you call a
man who only
eats casseroles ?

Stu !

What do you call a
Russian gardener ?

Ivanhoe !

What do you call
the woman who
fell off the white
cliffs ?

Eileen Dover !

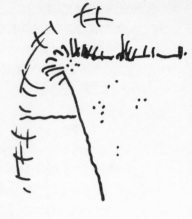

★

What do you call the red
Indian woman
who laughs at small cars ?

Minnie - Ha Ha !

★

What do you call a
girl with her own
sweet shop ?

Candy !

★

What would you
call a band that
your father joined ?

A Pop Group !

★

What do you call a man who dances in coal mines with hankies in his hands ?

A Morris Minor !

What do you call a girl who lives under the house ?

Cella !

What do you call a girl who lives in a jar ?

Jamima !

What do you call a man with a cat sat on his head ?

Matt !

What do you call a
teacher who
falls asleep in
the class ?

Nothing! You don't
want to wake him up !!

★

What do you call a chicken
that lays lightbulbs ?

A battery hen !

What does the invisible
man call his *mum* and *dad* ?

Transparents !

What was *Humpty Dumpty*
wearing the last time
you saw him ?

A Shell Suit !

What do you call a dead parrot ?

A Polygon !

What do you call an animal that eats weeds ?

Dan de Lion !

What do you call a ghost's horse ?

A Nightmare !

What do you call a dangerous woman who works in a cake shop ?

Tilly the bun !

What do you call a German who is afraid of small, confined spaces ?

Klaus Trophobia !

What do you call a man with a cactus on his head ?

Sandy !

What do you call a man with a wooden leg and a steak and kidney pudding on his shoulder ?

A Pierate !

What do you call a Roman emperor with a mouse on his head ?

Julius Cheeser !

What do you call a skeleton that refuses to do any work ?

Bone Idle !

What do you call a woman who sneezes all the
time and likes knock, knock jokes ?

Tish who ?!

What do you call a cat
in a chemists shop ?

Puss in Boots !

What do you call a part-time
petrol pump attendant?

Arthur Gallon !

What do you call a woman with
a chimney on her head ?

Ruth !

What do you call a man
with a lens cap on his head ?

Len !

What do you call a man
with a jumbo jet
on his head ?

Ron Way !

What do you call a
woman with a crown
on her head ?

Your Majesty !

School
Screams...

Teacher - You should have been here at nine o'clock this morning !

Pupil - Why, did something happen ?

English Teacher - Sally, do you like Kipling ?

Sally - I don't know, Sir, I've never eaten one !

My last school was so rough they didn't have a school photograph - they sent home identikit pictures instead !

Science Teacher - Gary, do you know what Copper Nitrate is ?

Gary - Yes Sir, it's what they pay policemen on night duty !

History Teacher - Martin, where would I find Hadrian's wall ?

Martin - Wherever Hadrian left it, Sir !

Maths Teacher - Carol, why have you brought a picture of Henry the eighth in with you ?

Carol - You told us to bring a ruler in with us today !

Teacher - name one of Noah's children.

Pupil - Joan of Arc ?

And... for all those who were late this morning because they stayed up to watch the football... we're going to make School more like football...

you will all stay behind and do extra time tonight as a penalty !

Maths teacher - Blenkinsop, can you tell me the 9 times table please ?

Blenkinsop - You asked me that yesterday, don't tell me you've forgotten it already !

Teacher - You're on English level 4 aren't you, Smith ?

Smith - Yes.

Teacher - Then take this English level 2 book for your father or he's never going to be able to catch up and do your homework properly !

Of course in my day you only had the one choice for school dinners....................

..............Like it or lump it !

★

Where do Martians go to train to be teachers ?

Mooniversity !

★

I think my maths teacher
is in love
with me...

How do you work
that out ?

...she puts red kisses all
over my homework !

★

What's the best
snake to take into a
maths lesson ?

An adder !

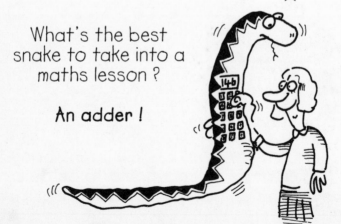

I would have done my homework, but.....

I didn't have any pocket money left, and my sister always demands cash in advance.....

My dad was working late, and he has all the brains in the family.....

My pen ran out and I spent all night looking for an inkwell.....

What is a history teacher's favourite fruit ?

Dates !

Please Miss, is it true that the French only ever eat one egg for breakfast ?

What makes you ask that ?

Because yesterday you said that in France, one egg is un oeuf !

Did you hear about the teacher who had to wear sunglasses in the classroom?

He had extremely bright pupils!

Anxious parent - What do you think my son will be when he has finished all his exams?

Teacher - An old age pensioner!

How many teachers does it take to work the photocopier?

Who cares, as long as it keeps them out of the classroom!

Head - You boy, stop running around like that! Don't you know who I am?

Pupil - There's a bloke here who doesn't even know who he is!

Why do swimming teachers like elephants ?

Because they never forget their trunks !

*We've got a new drama teacher -
she's a real class act !*

Head - That's Hodgkiss, the school bully.

Visitor - How dreadful, can't you do anything to stop him ?

Head - Certainly not, or I'd never get the teachers back to the classrooms after lunch break !

Who is a teacher's favourite actor ?

Michael Caine !

Eric should make an excellent train driver, as he has more experience of lines than any other pupil in the school !

Our cookery teacher knows his onions...

Our P.E. teacher thinks we're a real shower...

Our last maths teacher was taken away...

**Our music teacher never accepts notes
from home...**

Where do new teachers come from ?

They're produced on an assembly line !

What were the names of
the very first teachers ?

Miss and Sir !

Teacher - Is your father helping you with your
homework ?

Pupil - No, sir, if anything he knows even less
than I do !

Well, son, how did you find the maths exam ?

Unfortunately, it wasn't lost !

Teacher - Smith, give me a sentence with the word politics in it.

Smith - My pet parrot swallowed the alarm clock and now Polly ticks !

What's the best way to tell your maths teacher that you have forgotten to do your homework - again ?

From a great distance !

Teacher - If your father gave you £1.50 pocket money and your mother gave you £2.50, what would you have ?

Pupil - **Someone else's parents !**

★

Pupil - Do I need any qualifications to work as a Father Christmas in a department store ?

Careers teacher - **You need Ho ! Ho ! Ho ! levels !**

Teacher - Well, at least I know that no-one in the school football team will ever start smoking.

Head - How do you work that out ?

Teacher - **Because they always lose their matches !**

Our School cook was arrested for cruelty - she was caught beating eggs, battering fish fingers and whipping cream !

John - I bet our chemistry teacher could cure your insomnia mum...

Mum - Why, is he a doctor as well ?

John - **No, but as soon as he starts to speak half the class fall asleep !**

Teacher - Are you sending Gary to boarding school ?

Parent - **Yes. His report says he is always bored !**

Games Teacher - Read these books and they will help you get fit - they are exercise books !

We're going to build a bonfire, put our maths books on the top, put school dinners in the middle, and burn the bloomin' lot !

Teacher -How many letters in the alphabet ?

Pupil - 25 !

Teacher - How do you work that out ?

Pupil - Well, it's Christmas next week, so there's Noel !

Head - Why did you call Mulder and Scully into the school ?

Pupil - I looked into the school kitchen and saw an unidentified frying object !

Teacher -Jenkins, what's the difference between an elephant and my desk ?

Jenkins - Don't know sir.

Teacher - In that case I think I'll send someone else to put these books in my desk drawers !

51

Teacher -I just don't understand how one person can make so many mistakes in their homework !

Pupil -Oh I can't take all the credit, sir, my Dad did most of it !

We sent our teacher's photograph to a lonely hearts club...

They sent it straight back - they said they weren't THAT lonely !

How can you tell when a teacher is in a good mood ?

No, I don't know either !

What do you call a teacher with a pile of sports equipment on his head ?

Jim !

What do you call a man with a school on his head ?

Ed !

What do maths teachers do when their sinks get blocked ?

They work it out with a pencil !

What do cannibals have for school dinners ?

Snake and pygmy pie, with chimps and beings !

What do you call a boy who only just gets to school on time every day ?

Justin !

Did you hear about the maths teacher who wanted an Italian take away, but was divided about whether to have additional cheese !

★

Our technology teacher left to try and make something of himself !

Who's your favourite teacher ?

The Finnish one !

We haven't got any Finnish teachers !

Yes we have. Every day she says "Finish what you're doing and go home !

Mum - How did you do at school today ?

John - Great ! The teacher told me I was a moron !

Mum -And it's not as if you come from a religious family !

Steve - I wish MY dad would help me with my homework like yours does !

Joe - I wish your dad would help me as well. I got 3 out of 25 and another detention thanks to mine !

Teacher -
Blenkinsop. Can you tell me the 9 times table ? !

Blenkinsop -
If you don't know it at your age,
what chance have I got !

What do you get if you
cross a teacher and a
traffic warden ?

**Someone who gives
you 500 double yellow
lines for being late !**

New pupil -
Who is that over there wearing spurs
and a silver star and carrying a saddle
over his shoulder ?

Old pupil -
Oh! That's the Deputy Head !

What is the space alien's
favourite school subject ?

**Art - because he likes
to create Marsterpieces !**

Johnny -
Hey, Dad, I'll bet you can't write in the dark !

Dad -
Of course I can !

Johnny -
Good! I'll just turn out the light
and you can sign my school report !

★

Of course in my day we didn't have
computers to help us..................

..............we had to get our schoolwork
wrong all on our own !

★

Why do robot teachers never get scared ?

Because they have nerves of steel !

★

I think Johnny will make an excellent astronaut
when he leaves school...

Why do you think that ?

...because he's had nothing but
space between his ears all the
years he's been at this school !

Why are you taking the Queen into your exams ?

It's a maths exam, she's my ruler !

I would have done my homework, but.....

I used up all the ink in my pen
drawing the curtains.....

they didn't have any more copies of Romeo and
Juliet in the video library.....

you said to hand it in tomorrow - and I will.....

What is an English teacher's
favourite fruit ?

The Grapes of Wrath !

Please Miss, is it true that in the future all trains and buses will run on time ?

What makes you ask that ?

Because my dad says that they will still run on petrol !

Did you hear about the cross eyed teacher who had to retire ?

He couldn't control his pupils !

He must have been related to the one-eyed teacher who also had to retire...

...because he didn't have enough pupils

What's the difference between a teacher and a mouse ?

They're like chalk and cheese !

How many teachers does it take to change a lightbulb ?

One, if it's a free period. 17, if it's a lesson !

Head -
I understand you're interested in a career in languages ?

Pupil -
Yes, sir, my English teacher says I speak perfect gobledygook!

Why are maths teachers good at solving detective stories ?

Because they can tell when all the clues add up !

We have a new Italian teacher -
I'll bet she pasta lot of exams to get this job !

What is a robot teacher's favourite part of the day ?

Assembly !

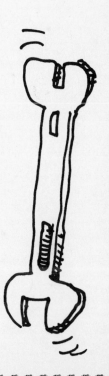

Why did you give an apple to our exchange werewolf teacher from Transylvania ?

Because I wanted to be creature's pet !

★

Our cookery teacher **grills** anyone who fails to hand in their homework...

Our P.E. teacher thinks we're all **good sports**...

Our maths teacher gives us **additional** homework...

Our music teacher makes a real **song and dance** when we're late for class...

★

Where do vampire teachers come from ?

Teacher Draining College !

★

Where do vampire teachers like to work ?

In the school necks door !

Teacher - Have you been stupid all your life ?

Pupil - Not yet !

Your son is so dim, he doesn't even know where Hadrian's Wall is !

Well, if Hadrian lost it what has that got to do with our Cedric !

Teacher - Smith, give me a sentence with the word indifferent in it !

Smith -
My television doesn't work anymore since I plugged the aerial indifferent !

What's the easiest way to get a day off school ?

Wait until Saturday !!

Teacher -
If you had 50p in each trouser pocket, and £1 in each blazer pocket what would you have ?

Pupil - Someone else's uniform !

Pupil -
Do I need any
qualifications to
work as a vet ?

Careers teacher -
No, you've had plenty of experience with animals
already - I've seen the rest of your class !

Teacher -
The school cook has been caught soaking
the eggs in whisky again !

Head -
What on earth was she doing that for ?

Teacher -
Because she wanted to serve scotch eggs !

I think you've been built upside down Blenkinsop !
Why do you think that sir ?
Because your feet smell and your nose runs !!

John - We've started a school fencing team !

Mum - Do you need any equipment ?

John - A paintbrush and some creosote !

Teacher -
Your son is rather troublesome in class, did he go to a good school before he started here ?

Parent -
Oh Yes, it was approved !

Teacher - Why are you taking those trainers into your exam ?

Pupil - I'm hoping to jog my memory !

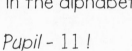

Teacher - How many letters in the alphabet ?

Pupil - 11 !

Teacher - How do you work that out ?

Pupil - t - h - e - a - l - p - h - a - b - e - t !

Head - Why do you want to take your science exam outside ?

Pupil - Because the truth is out there !

Teacher - Jenkins, what's the difference between a fairy story and the excuses you give me for not doing your maths homework ?

Jenkins - Don't know sir.

Teacher - A fairy story is believable !

Teacher - Be honest, Smith, what do you think this homework is worth ?

Pupil -Well, I paid £3.50 to Steven Blenkinsop for it !?

They tell me that my schooldays will be the happiest of my life, but they haven't met the matron here, the cook or the headmaster's wife !

Here's your chemistry exam paper Blenkinsop - totally unhurt !

What do you mean totally unhurt ?

I mean there's not a mark on it !!

What do you call a teacher
with a pile of bricks
on his head ?

The Housemaster !

★

Why can you always believe
what a teacher
with a beard tells you ?

They can't tell bare faced lies !

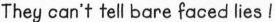

★

**That new monster teacher is terrible - Jim was
late yesterday and he bit his head off !**

★

Did you hear about the cannibal teacher...

**All his pupils were all late,
and now they're all ate !?**

★

I saw my history teacher in
town last night...
...he was out on a date !
...his girlfriend is a
history teacher as well...
...they go to a restaurant
and talk about old times !!

Did you hear about the Spanish teacher
looking for a job -

She castanet far and wide !

Glory, glory alleluyah
teacher hit me with a ruler
the ruler broke in two and
so she hit me with her shoe
and I wish I was at home...

Blenkinsop -Wwhat's the
easiest way to make a fire
using two sticks ?

Make sure one of them
is a match, sir !

Carol - When was Rome built ?

Well, it must have been at night because I know
Rome wasn't built in a day !

Blenkinsop - What type of musical instrument
did the early Britons play ?

The Anglo Saxophone ?

I want to be a jockey,
what qualifications will I need ?

Three Hay levels !

Our teacher put his
sunglasses on when he
gave out our
examination results
today...

**..he took a very dim
view of our
performance !**

When our science teacher retired we bought her
a bottle of toilet water - it cost £15 !

**What !? You could have had some water from
our toilet and I would only have charged you
£2.50 !!**

Smith - How do you make a hot cross bun ?

Pour hot water down a rabbit warren, sir !

Blenkinsop -
Why did Robin Hood steal from the rich ?

**Because the poor didn't have anthing
worth stealing !**

How does a maths teacher know how long she
sleeps ?

Because she takes a ruler to bed with her !

Knock, Knock...

Knock, Knock...
Who's there ?
Giraffe...
Giraffe Who ?
Giraffe to sit in front of me
at the cinema ?

Knock, knock...
Who's there ?
Amanda...
Amanda who ?
Amanda last step - open the door !

Knock, knock...
Who's there ?
Dell...
Dell who ?
Dell never know I was here if you don't tell them !

Knock, knock...
Who's there ?
Toodle...
Toodle who ?
Where are you going - I only just got here !

Knock, knock...
Who's there ?
Paul...
Paul who ?
Paul the door open and you'll see !

Knock Knock...
Who's there ?
Joanna...
Joanna who ?
**Joanna stop asking stupid questions
and let me in !**

★

Knock Knock...
Who's there ?
Ant...
Ant who ?
Ant I told you already ?

★

Knock Knock Knock...
Who's there ?
Moses...
Moses who ?
Moses if I knock 3 times you'll let me in !

★

Knock Knock...
Who's there ?
Corah...
Corah who ?
Corah wish I had a front door like this !

★

Knock Knock...
Who's there ?
Kent...
Kent who ?
Kent you fix the doorbell ?

Knock Knock...
Who's there ?
Yul...
Yul who ?
**Yul never know if you don't
open the door will you ? !**

Knock Knock...
Who's there ?
**Your maths teacher...
hello...hello....Is anyone
there...?**

Knock Knock...
Who's there ?
Isabel...
Isabel who ?
**Isabel a legal
requirement on a bicycle ?**

Knock Knock...
Who's there ?
Superman...
Superman who ?
You know I can't reveal my secret identity !

Knock Knock...
Who's there ?
Dooby Doobid...
Dooby Doobid who ?
Ah ! A Frank Sinatra fan !

★

Knock Knock...
Who's there ?
Doctor...
Doctor who ?
Have you seen my Tardis !?

Knock Knock...
Who's there ?
Tish...
Tish who ?
Bless you !

Knock Knock...
Who's there ?
Twitter...
Twitter who ?
You got an owl in there ?

Knock Knock...
Who's there ?
Cook...
Cook who ?
That's the first one I've heard this year !

Knock Knock...
Who's there ?
Snow...
Snow who ?
**Snow joke being out here
in the cold, let me in !**

Knock Knock...
Who's there ?
Nona...
Nona who ?
Nona your business !

Knock Knock...
Who's there ?
Adolf...
Adolf who ?
Adolf ball hit me in de mouf !

Knock Knock...
Who's there ?
Alec...
Alec who ?
Alec to see you guess !

Knock Knock...
Who's there ?
Les...
Les who ?
Les cut the small talk - just open the door !

★

Knock Knock...
Who's there ?
Wendy...
Wendy who ?
Wendy red red robin goes bob bob
bobbin along...

Knock Knock...
Who's there ?
Guess...
Guess who ?
Hang on, haven't we got this mixed up
somehow ?

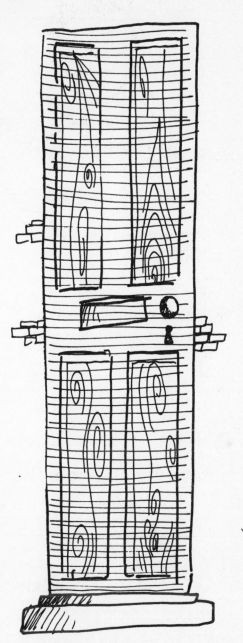

Knock Knock...
Who's there ?
Kungf...
Kungf who ?
**No need to
threaten me !**

Knock Knock...
Who's there ?
Marky...
Marky who ?
**Markys stuck in
the keyhole,
can you open it
from your side ?**

Knock Knock...
Who's there ?
Knock Knock...
Who's there ?
Knock Knock...
Just a minute I'll
open the door -
Yes, can I help you ?
**I've called to
collect my new
hearing aid !**

Knock Knock...
Who's there ?
Police...
Police who ?
Police let me in, I'm freezing out here !

Knock Knock...
Who's there ?
Pat...
Pat who ?
Actually it's Steve, I was just doing
an impersonation of Pat !

Knock Knock...
Who's there ?
Joe...
Joe who ?
Joe always have to
ask me that question ?

Knock Knock...
Who's there ?
The Cilla...
The Cilla who ?
The Cilla beggar who's
forgotten her key again !

Knock Knock...
Who's there?
Your maths teacher...
This is a recording...there's no one here
at the moment!

Knock Knock...
Who's there?
Jim...
Jim who?
Jim mind if I stay here tonight?

★

Knock Knock...
Who's there?
Aliens...
Aliens who?
**Just how many
Aliens
do you know?**

Knock Knock...
Who's there ?
Boo...
Boo who ?
No need to get upset, it's only a game !

Knock Knock...
Who's there ?
Mike...
Mike who ?
**Mike car won't start, can I
come in and phone the RAC ?**

Knock Knock...
Who's there ?
Carol...
Carol who ?
**Carol singers - you must
have heard us we've been
at it for 20 minutes !**

Knock Knock...
Who's there ?
Phil...
Phil who ?
Phil this bag with money,
I'm a burglar !

★

Knock Knock...
Who's there ?
The man from next door...
The man from next door who ?
The man from next door who has clearly come
home to the wrong house, sorry !

Knock Knock...
Who's there ?
Luke...
Luke who ?
Luke, stop messing about
and let me in !

Knock Knock...
Who's there ?
Alec...
Alec who ?
Alec your front door !

Knock Knock...
Who's there ?
Haydn...
Haydn who ?
Haydn like it at all !

Knock Knock...
Who's there ?
Ivan...
Ivan who ?
Ivan to come in - open the door !

Knock Knock...
Who's there ?
Josie...
Josie who ?
Josie any reason to keep me waiting out here ?

Knock Knock...
Who's there ?
The Spice Girls...
Come in, come in, how rude of me to keep you
waiting...

Knock Knock...
Who's there ?
Jeanie...
Jeanie who ?
Jeanie comprend pas - je suis Francais !

Knock Knock...
Who's there ?
Bill...
Bill who ?
Bill-ieve it or not this is a joke !

Knock Knock...
Who's there ?
Bert...
Bert who ?
Bert surely you recognise my voice !

Knock Knock...
Who's there ?
Ernie...
Ernie who ?
Ernie chance of you opening the door ?

Knock Knock...
Who's there ?
Norman...
Norman who ?
**Norman gets past this door
without your permission do they ? !**

Knock Knock...
Who's there ?
Ivor...
Ivor who ?
Ivor key of my own now !

Knock, knock...
Who's there ?
Ken...
Ken who ?
Ken I please come in now I want to play
something else ?

Knock, Knock...
Who's there ?
Avenue !
Avenue who ?
Avenue guessed yet ?

Knock Knock...
Who's there ?
Joke...
Joke who ?
Joke keep everyone waiting this long ?

Knock Knock...
Who's there ?
Bert...
Bert who ?
Bert you'll never guess !?

Knock, knock...
Who's there ?
The Witch...
The Witch who ?
Bless you !

Knock, knock...
Who's there ?
Maddona...
Maddona who ?
Maddona have to stand out here all night !

Knock, knock...
Who's there ?
Gunga Din...
Gunga Din who ?
Gunga Din the door's locked !

Knock, knock...
Who's there ?
Nige...
Nige who ?
Nige who believe it's me ?

Knock Knock...
Go away ! I'm reading
the next section !

Knock Knock...
Who's there ?
Colin...
Colin Who ?
Colin me names is going to get
you into big trouble !

★

Knock Knock...
Who's there ?
Aidan...
Aida who ?
Aidan idea you would ask that !

★

Knock Knock...
Who's there ?
Frank...
Frank who ?
Frankenstein !

Knock Knock...
Who's there ?
Geezer...
Geezer who ?
**Geezer couple of minutes and
I'll pick this lock !**

Knock Knock...
Who's there ?
Tim...
Tim who ?
T-I-M-B-E-R !@*!!

Knock Knock...
Who's there ?
Jack...
Jack who ?
**Jack my car up will you,
I want to fix the exhaust !**

Knock Knock...
Who's there ?
L.E....
L.E. who ?
L.E. Funt !

Knock Knock...
Who's there ?
Kipper...
Kipper who ?
Kipper your hands off
my ice cream !

Knock Knock...
Who's there ?
Dinah...
Dinah who ?
Dinahsaur!

Knock Knock...
Who's there ?
Vlad...
Vlad who ?
Vlad a long time you take
to answer the door !

JINGLE
JINGLE

Knock Knock...
Who's there ?
Paul...
Paul who ?
Paul the other leg,
it's got bells on !

Knock Knock...
Who's there ?
Carl...
Carl who ?
Carl this a warm reception !?

Knock Knock...
Who's there ?
Oomaht...
Oomaht who ?
Have you dropped something on your foot ?

Knock Knock...
Who's there ?
Jess...
Jess who ?
**Jess open the door will
you !!**

Knock Knock...
Who's there ?
Snow...
Snow who ?
**Snow use - I can't
remember !**

Knock Knock...
Who's there ?
Ivor...
Ivor who ?
**Ivor got my fingers stuck
in your letter flap !**

Knock Knock...
Who's there ?
Apple...
Apple who ?
Apple the door too hard and
hit myself in the nose !

★

Knock Knock...
Who's there ?
Only Joe...
Only Joe who ?
Only Joking,
it's me really !

★

Knock Knock...
Who's there ?
Timbukt...
Timbukt who ?
That's right !
How can you
see through a
solid door !!

★

Knock Knock...
Who's there ?
Pop...
Pop who ?
Pop round and unlock the back door -
my wellies are all muddy !

Knock Knock...
Who's there ?
Laetitia...
Laetitia who ?
Crikey, sounds like your
cold has turned into flu !

Knock Knock...
Who's there ?
Wee Spencer...
Wee Spencer who ?
Wee spencer long
out here
waiting we're
freezing !

Knock Knock...
Who's there ?
Kurt...
Kurt who ?
Kurt out that last joke - it's terrible !

★

Knock Knock...
Who's there ?
Dennis...
Dennis who ?
Dennis must be
the right place
- he said you'd
ask that !

★

Knock Knock...
Who's there ?
Tinkerbell...
Tinkerbell who ?
Tinkerbell would save me having to
do all this knocking !

★

Knock Knock...
Who's there ?
Chester...
Chester who ?
Chester man delivering a parcel !

Knock Knock...
Who's there ?
A. Roland...
A. Roland who ?
**A Roland butter
would be very nice -
do you have any !**

Knock Knock...
Who's there ?
Ouvrez...
Ouvrez who ?
Ouvrez la porte, sil-te-plait !

Knock Knock...
Who's there ?
Gordon...
Gordon who ?
Gordon tired of standing
here I can tell you !

★

Knock Knock...
Who's there ?
Luke...
Luke who ?
Luke through the little
spyglass and you'll see !

★

Knock Knock...
Who's there ?
June...
June who ?
June know how long I've
been waiting out here ?!

Knock Knock...
Who's there ?
Creatures from another dimension...
Creatures from another dimension who ?
Creatures from another dimension who are
getting tired of waiting to be let in, earthling !

Knock Knock...
Who's there ?
Witch Doctor...
Witch Doctor who ?
The one in the floppy
hat and long scarf !

Knock Knock...
Who's there ?
Ooh Ooh Ooh...
Ooh Ooh Ooh who ?
Stop playing at fire engines
and let me in !

Knock Knock...
Who's there ?
Paul...
Paul who ?
**Paul the door from your side -
it seems to be stuck !**

★

Knock Knock...
Who's there ?
Bart...
Bart who ?
**Bart time you
opened the door !**

★

Knock Knock...
Who's there ?
Daniel...
Daniel who ?
**Daniel be coming round
in a bit, so leave
the door open !**

★

Knock Knock...
Who's there ?
Wanda...
Wanda who ?
Wanda know how much
longer you're going
to keep me hanging
around out here !

★

Knock Knock...
Who's there ?
Atilla...
Atilla who ?
Atilla you open dis door
I'ma gonna stand here !

★

Knock Knock...
Who's there ?
Howill...
Howill who ?
Howill you have your
egg - fried, boiled or
scrambled ?

Knock Knock...
Who's there ?
Amos...
Amos who ?
Amosquito !

Knock Knock...
Who's there ?
Little old lady...
Little old lady who ?
Your yodelling is getting better all the time !

Knock Knock...
Who's there ?
Al...
Al who ?
Al live here - so let me in !

Knock Knock...
Who's there ?
McKee...
McKee who ?
McKee doesn't fit !

Knock Knock...
Who's there ?
Fancy...
Fancy who ?
Fancy meeting you here !

Knock Knock...
Who's there ?
Phillipa...
Phillipa who ?
**Phillipa hot bath - I've
just fallen in the mud !**

Knock Knock...
Who's there ?
Dismay...
Dismay who ?
**Dismay be the last time
I come round here !**

Knock Knock...
Who's there ?
Ivan...
Ivan who ?
Ivan idea you already know !

Knock Knock...
Who's there ?
Mouse...
Mouse who ?
Mouse has burned down -
I'm coming to stay with you !

★

Knock, Knock...
Who's there ?
Shirley
Shirley who ?
Shirley we don't have to go through this
rigmarole everytime I come home from work !

Knock Knock...
Who's there ?
Len...
Len who ?
**Len me a key and I won't have to knock any
more !**

Knock Knock...
Who's there ?
Izzy...
Izzy who ?
Izzy ever going to fit a doorbell ?!

Knock Knock...
Who's there ?
Carlos...
Carlos who ?
**Carlos sometime and we'll arrange
a game of football !**

Knock, Knock...
Who's there ?
Gladice...
Gladice who ?
**Gladice nice weather if you're going to keep
me waiting out here all day !**

Knock Knock...
Who's there ?
Vera...
Vera who ?
Vera the right keys ?!

Knock Knock...
Who's there ?
Lewis...
Lewis who ?
Lewis doorknob's
come
off in my hand !

Knock Knock...
Who's there ?
Dinner...
Dinner who ?
Dinner where
me key is !

Knock, Knock...
Who's there ?
Jester...
Jester who ?
Jester minute - this is my house - what
are you doing in there !

Animal Antics...

Looks like Reindeer !

What do you call a goat who robs banks ?

Billy the Kid !

If cows get milked - what do goats get ?

Butted !

*If a house mouse sleeps in a house
and a field mouse sleeps in a field
do dormice sleep in dorms ?*

Where do rabbits go when they want
something to read ?

Buck Shops !

Rabbit - How do I know this TV will work when
I get it home ?

Shopkeeper -It comes with a full Warrenty !

Name a comedian that dogs really like...

...Ronnie Barker !

Why do elephants
paint their toenails
red ?

**So they can hide in
Cherry trees !**

Hickory Dickory Dock,
The horse ran up the clock.

Anybody need any firewood ?

Why is the sky so high ?

So birds don't bump their heads !

What goes... 'Now you see me, now you don't ?'

A Zebra using a pelican crossing !

★

What will you get if you sit under a cow ?

A pat on the head !

When Mary had a little lamb
The doctor was surprised
But when Old Macdonald had a farm
He couldn't believe his eyes !

What do porcupines eat with their cheese ?

Prickled onions !

What do you get if you cross a cow with a camel ?

Lumpy custard !

How do you stop rabbits digging up your garden ?

Easy - take their spades away !

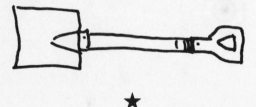

Why don't polar bears eat penguins ?

They can't get the wrappers off !

We call our dog Blacksmith because every now and again he makes a bolt for the door !

Why are you taking that snake into the maths exam ?

It's an adder !

How many elephants can you get into a Mini ?

Four. 2 in the front seats and 2 in the back seats !

How many hippos can you get into a Mini ?

Four ?

Don't be silly ! There are 4 elephants in it already !

Amateur Lion Taming

by

Claude Bottom

What do you call an elephant in a telephone box ?

Whatever you like - it will be stuck so it can't chase you !

★

What goes 'Mark, Mark...'

A dog with a swollen lip !

★

What are baby crabs called ?

Nippers !

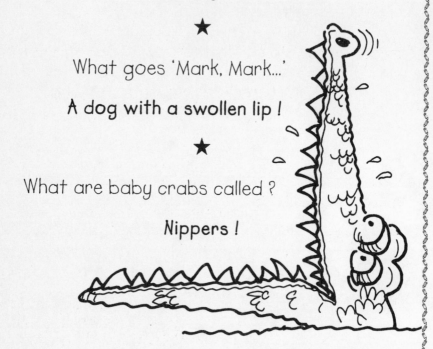

Waiter - Bring me a crocodile sandwich....
....and make it snappy !

Did you hear about the Shetland Pony who was asked to leave the animal choir ?

She was always a little horse !

Police are looking for a criminal octopus...

He is well armed and dangerous !

What lies at the bottom of the sea and shivers ?

A nervous wreck !

What's the fastest fish in the lake ?

A motor Pike !

What does your cat eat for breakfast ?

Mine eats Mice Crispies !

Did you know that alligators eat beans for breakfast ?

Human Beans of course !

HUMAN
BEANS
IN
TOMATO
SAUCE

Noah's Ark was able to find its way about at night because it had been fitted with floodlights !

★

Why do bees hum ?

Because they have forgotten the words !

Where do you take an injured bee ?

To the waspital !

...just as you would take an injured pony to the horsepital !

Why do railway porters like elephants ?

Because they always carry their own trunks !

What has 10 legs, three heads but only two arms ?

A man and a dog sitting on a zebra !

What's grey and zooms through the jungle at 70 miles an hour ?

An elephant on a motor bike !

Why should you never play cards for money in the jungle ?

Because there are too many Cheetahs about !

What vegetable do you get if you cross a sheepdog with a bunch of daffodils ?

A collie - flower !

What bird lights up the farmyard at night ?

A battery hen !

113

What game do ponies play ?

Stable tennis !

Why did the hedgehog cross the road ?

He wanted to see his flat mate !

Why did the dinosaur cross the road ?

Because chickens hadn't been invented
in those days !

Why did the cat cross the road ?

To see his friend who worked in the
chemists - Puss in Boots !

Why did the snake
cross the road ?

Because it couldn't use
the footbridge !

Why was the haddock too scared
to use a crossing to cross the road ?

**Because someone told him that
pelicans eat fish !**

Why did the duck cross the road ?

It was the chicken's day off !

What do schools of mackerel do before an
exam ?

Re - fish - ion !

Why do elephants have wrinkles ?

Because they hate ironing !

How do you know if an elephant has
been in your fridge ?

They leave footprints in the butter !

What creature comes in handy in the car ?

A windscreen Viper !

Why didn't the young cat get into trouble for telling lies ?

He was only kitten !

What is yellow and very dangerous ?

Shark infested custard !
or
A laser powered banana !

What does it mean if you find a set of horse shoes ?

Some poor horse is walking around in his socks !

Where do kangaroos go for an eye test ?

To the hoptician !

I can't do it, you can't do it, the farmer can't do it...

...what is it ?

Milk chocolate !

Another name for parrot food - **pollyfilla !**

Did you hear about the dog who was too lazy to dig up his bone ?

He was bone idle !

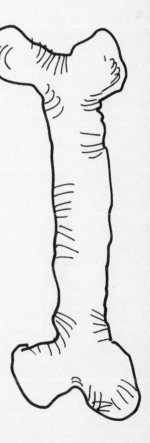

How many sheep does it take to make a sweater ?

I didn't even know that sheep could knit !

Why are elephants grey ?

So you can tell them apart from strawberries !

Why does a giraffe have such a long neck ?

Have you ever smelled a giraffe's feet !?

Bullfighting
for
beginners

by

Matt. A. Dores

When sheep are cold they gather in a big circle and a few sheep in the centre make a lot of noise and this keeps everyone else warm...

...this is called central bleating !

What do the police have to have before they can come into your home looking for escaped parrots ?

A perch warrant !

What do you call a sheep with a machine gun ?

Lambo !

What does a cat rest his head on in bed ?

A caterpiller !

What sort of cat sells wood ?

A Catalogue !

What part of a car can be used to change cats into something else ?

The catalytic converter !

What bulls hide on the riverbank waiting to charge at you ?

Bullrushes !

If you go to the doctor because you are a little hoarse, what is he likely to give you ?

Cough Stirrup !

Which dog is always making mistakes ?

A cock-up spaniel !

What is a cat's favourite TV programme ?

The Mews at Ten !

I'd like a tube of cat glue please !

What on earth is that for ?

Well, I always thought that cats came in one piece - but someone told me you have to buy them as kits !

What was the title of the Shakespeare play about pigs ?

Hamlet !

Why do elephants paint the soles of
their feet yellow ?

So they can hide upside down in custard !

★

Hickory Dickory Dock,
Three mouse ran up the clock.

The clock struck one...
...the other two got out of the
way just in time !

 ★

Why is the sky blue ?

So birds know they're not flying upside down !

What is the correct name for a water otter ?

A kettle !

What's green and highly dangerous ?

A frog with a machine gun !

BURP...

Mary had a little lamb
she also had a horse
for the horse
she made a saddle
for the lamb
she made mint sauce !

Is that budgie expensive ?

No, sir, it's going cheep !

CHEEP!

What do you get if you cross
a cow with a child and a pub ?

The milky bar kid !

What is blue and swings through the trees ?

A chimpanzee in a boiler suit !

When is it bad luck to have a
black cat cross your path ?

When you are a mouse !

What is the difference
between an apple and
an elephant ?

Apples are green !

What's the best way to
catch a mouse ?

**Get someone to throw
one at you !**

How many elephants does it take to change a lightbulb ?

Four! One to hold the bulb and three to turn the stepladder !

What lives on a ship and says 'croak, croak!' when it's foggy ?

A Froghorn !

What do you call a rich trendy elephant ?

A member of the jumbo jet set !

Why do eagles go to church ?

Because they are birds of prey !

What do mouse jokers like doing best ?

Taking the Mickey !

What do you call a vampire pig ?

Frankenswine !

Did you hear about the four elephants who bought a mini so they could play their favourite game... ?

...squash !

How can you possibly be the school swot - you're the least intelligent person I know ?

I know, but I go round killing all the flies !

What do you call a dog that runs up the M1 at 70 miles an hour ?

A two litre Rover !

What do you call two pigs that live together ?

Pen pals !

What is the highest form of animal life ?

A giraffe !

★

Have you changed the water in the goldfish bowl ?

No, they haven't drunk the water I put in yesterday yet !

★

What do you call a horse that sunbathes behind a venetian blind ?

A zebra !

★

What do you call a nervous insect ?

A jitterbug !

★

Why couldn't the butterfly get into the dance ?

Because it was a moth ball !

★

What do you get if you cross a giraffe
and a dog ?

**An animal that chases low flying
aeroplanes instead of cars !**

What is the difference
between a skunk
and a squirrel ?

**Skunks don't know how to
operate a deodorant spray !**

What vegetable do you get if you cross a
sheepdog with a plate of jelly ?

The Collie - wobbles !

Your dog must be really intelligent
if he can play scrabble !

Nah! He never wins !

What animal do you
eat for pudding ?

Moose !

Why did the hedgehog cross the road ?

He was competing in a point to point race !

Name four animals from the dog family ...

Mummy dog, daddy dog and two puppies !

Is it true that you can speak
in cat language ?

Me - How ?

Which football team do most
snakes support ?

Slitherpool !

How does a fish teacher keep
control of a rowdy class ?

She puts everyone in their plaice !

Why did the duck cross the
motorway at rush hour ?

I don't know, it must have
been quackers !

What is the most
valuable fish ?

The goldfish !

Why do elephants never get phone bills ?

Because they get free trunk calls !

What weighs over 1000 kilos and wears
flowers in its hair ?

A Hippy - potamous !

What sort of American holidays
do animals take ?

They fly jumbo jets to Moo York !

What is green and very dangerous ?

A 12 bore cucumber !

What did the chicken say when the farmer
grabbed it by the tail feathers ?

Oh, no! This is the end of me !!

What is a kangaroo's
favourite cowboy hero ?

Hopalong Cassidy !

What is a kangaroo's favourite
playground game ?

Hopscotch !

What is a kangaroo's
favourite sporting event ?

The hop-stacle race !

How do sheep block the
entrance to their fields ?

With a five baaa gate !

Why are elephants grey ?

**Because red paint doesn't
come in big enough tins !**

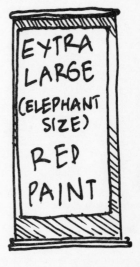

What is a vampire's favourite animal ?

The giraffe - because it has such a long neck !

What has one horn, and gives
fresh milk every day ?

A milk lorry !

Why are you selling parrots fitted with
little alarm clocks ?

**Because my wife told me I should
go into politics !**

What do the police call their dogs
when they have a cold ?

Sniffer dogs !

What do you call a pig with a machine gun !

Hambo !

What sort of cow
wears a jumper ?

A jersey !

What sort of dog wears gloves ?

A boxer !

Monster
Madness...

Eat your sprouts, they'll put
colour in your cheeks.

But I don't want green cheeks !

What do vampires play every week ?

The National Clottery !

What should you take if a monster
invites you for dinner ?

Someone who can't run as fast as you !

Why do vampires have to
write so many letters ?

**They have to reply to their
fang clubs !**

What sort of monster wakes you up in the
morning with a nice cup of tea ?

A mummy !

Why are ghosts so bad at telling lies ?

Because you can always see through them !

The Haunted House

by

Hugo First

Mummy, what is a vampire ?

**Be quiet dear and drink your blood
before it clots !**

What do you call an evil,
8 foot tall, green,
hairy monster ?

Whatever he tells you to !

What is a monster's favourite handicraft ?

Tie and Die !

What do monsters do at parties ?

**They eat I scream and jelly babies
and play haunt the thimble !**

Did you see that wolf ?

Where ?

No, it was just an ordinary one !

What's the name of that very
scary all girl band ?

You mean the Spice Ghouls !

It's no good locking your door - monsters can
always get in !

They have a set of skeleton keys !

Doctor, said the cannibal, I have this terrible stomach ache !

You must have eaten someone who disagreed with you !

A vampire's coffin fell off the back of a lorry and started rolling down a steep hill. The vampire knew exactly what to do. He went into a local chemist and asked if they had any sore throat sweets to stop his coffin !

Where do vampires keep their savings ?

In a blood bank !

Did you hear about the baby monster who had hundreds of little holes all over his face ?

He was learning to eat with a fork !

Why do vampires take their football so seriously ?

Because there is always so much at stake !

Where do ghosts practise frightening people ?

At swooniversity !

What do ghosts write their letters on?

Type - frighters !

How do mummies keep a secret ?

They keep it under wraps !

What do you call a monster who never blows his nose ?

The bogeyman !

Why do skeletons rub themselves all over with towels when they've been swimming ?

To get bone dry !

What is a sea monsters favourite takeaway ?

Fish and ships with worry sauce !

I know a vampire who spends all morning writing letters...

Well, he has to reply to his fang mail !

Menu

Shepherd Pie

or

Ploughman Lunch

followed by

Necktarines with double scream

What's the difference between a monster and an omelette ?

One is full of yolks, the other full of folks !

What sort of horses do monsters ride?

Night mares !

When a monster's hungry and needs to be fed,
it's no good hiding under the bed !
He'll roll you in the mattress,
till you're buried like a mole,
then chomp you down in two big bites,
like a giant sausage roll !

Why was the monster's head sticky ?

Because he styled his hair with a honey comb !

What did the monster say when it saw someone going past on a mountain bike ?

Ah ! Meals on wheels !

What is a vampire's favourite soup ?

Scream of mushroom !

Monster - Waiter, this is ordinary spaghetti - I ordered worms !

Waiter - Ah, I wondered why the man on the table next to you was being sick in the toilet !

Sally - What is the difference between a monster and a digestive biscuit ?

Jim - I don't know.

Sally - Have you ever tried dunking a monster in your tea?

A ghost went into a pub at midnight and asked the barman for a whisky. "Sorry sir," replied the barman, "we aren't allowed to serve spirits after closing time."

Party games for monsters...

Pass the person
and
swallow the leader !

What sort of monsters have wavy hair ?

Sea monsters !

What do you have to get if you invite monsters round to your house for a party ?

A new house !

Which railway company employs ghosts ?

British Wail !

(They work as in-spectres)

What do Hungarian ghosts eat ?

Ghoulash !

What position does ghosts play
in football teams ?

Ghoulkeepers !

What do you call a relaxed ghost ?

Ghoul as a cucumber !

What do you call a haunted set square ?

A trian-ghoul !

Where do ghouls go for their holidays
and how do they get there ?

**They fly British Scareways to
the Isle of Fright !**

Why do travelling salesmen always try to
sell things to vampires ?

Because they know they are suckers !

Where was Frankenstein's head made ?

Bolton !

Why does Dracula wear bright red braces ?

To hold his trousers up !

What sound do baby ghosts make when they cry ?

Boo Hoo !
or
they wail !

★

What is the first thing a vampire sinks his fangs into after the dentist has sharpened and polished them ?

The dentist's neck !

★

What do ghostly boy scouts sing round the camp fire ?

Ging - gang - ghouly - ghouly - ghouly - ghouly - gotcha !

★

Why are ghosts no good at telling lies ?

Because you can always see through them !

★

Who was one of James Bond's spooky enemies ?

Ghouldfinger !

What sort of vampires prey on elephants ?

The very stupid ones !

What do ghosts do in the countryside ?

They go fox haunting !

What do you do to keep ghosts fit ?

Call in an exercisist !

*A new ghost was sitting in bed reading
when an old ghost walked through the wall
and into his room.
"It's no good,' said the new ghost, "I still don't
understand how you do it"*
**"Watch," said the old ghost, "and I'll go
through it again !"**

★

What tune to ghosts sing their babies
to sleep with ?

Ghoulden slumbers !

What is a monster's favourite game?

Hide and Shriek!

I'd tell you the story of the vampire's broken tooth...

...but there's no point!

Why aren't robots afraid of monsters?

Because they have nerves of steel!

Did you hear about the witch who was caught speeding on her broomstick?

She had a brush with the law!

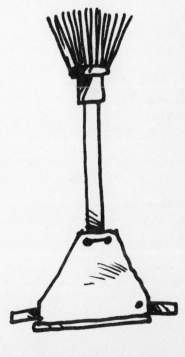

What is a monster's favourite shape ?

A vicious circle !

What do you think when
you see a monster ?

'I hope he hasn't
seen me !'

Where do monsters send
their dirty washing ?

The dry screamers !

and they send it in a hauntry basket !

Why do skeletons
love Doctor McCoy
on Star Trek ?

Because he's called
bones too !

What do monsters read in the
newspaper every morning ?

Their horror - scope !

What do you call a
monster with
a wooden leg ?

Long John Slither !

What is a vampire's
favourite
convenience food ?

Black pudding !

What do baby monsters sometimes
suffer from ?

Chicken spooks !

149

Why do vampire families never fight ?

Because they can't stand bad blood !

Where do ghosts read the news ?

In a whhhooooosspaper !

What do ghosts leave their
children when they die ?

All their unwordly goods !

★

What sort of music do
mummies like best ?

Wrap music !

★

What do you call a vampire who spends all
his time in the pub ?

Count Drunkula !

Why do skeletons not trust archaeologists ?

Because they indulge in skullduggery !

What is a sea monsters favourite toy ?

A sea-saw !

⭐

Gnomes have dreadful table manners...

...they are always Goblin their food !

Menu
Sean cocktail
or
Dawn on the cob
followed by
I Scream !
(and so would you if you had been there !)

A werewolf can't die
a vampire can fly
a monster can bite off your head.
It's no wonder I'm scared'
cos the noise I just heard...

means they're all hiding under my bed !

What TV proramme do monsters watch ?

'Glad He Ate Us' !

What is the best way to let a vampire know
he's not welcome at your party ?

**Offer him a garlic sausage sandwich
in a hot cross bun, and tell him
there is stake to follow !**

What sort of pets do monsters keep ?

Ghould - fish !

★

What did the vampire say when it saw the queue at the doctor's surgery ?

Necks please !

★

What is a monster's favourite soup ?

Any flavour, as long as it's a hearty meal !

★

Monster - What is that smoke coming from the kitchen ?

Waiter - Well, you asked us to fry you a vicar - that's holy smoke !

★

Sally - Did you make a sandwich with half a
monster in it ?

Jim - certainly not !

Sally - Oh! Then you must have
eaten half already !

How can you help a
starving monster ?

Give him a hand !

What can you buy
a monster to
decorate
his Christmas tree ?

Furry lights !

Why do monsters let out a
blood curdling scream ?

Because otherwise it would be too runny
to spread on their sandwiches !

What do monsters take
to a house warming party ?

Matches !

Which shop
employs ghosts ?

Marks & Spectres

What magazine do houseproud
monsters read ?

Ghouled Housekeeping !

What do monster football fans sing ?

Ghoul never walk alone !

★

Why does Cinderella play football so badly ?

**Well, so would you if you had
a pumpkin for a coach !**

How can you tell if a monster is friendly ?

Give him a sandwich and see if he bites the hand that feeds him !

★

What is the essential feature on a witches computer ?

The Spell-checker !

★

Monster - How much are those kittens in the window ?

Pet shop owner - Twelve pounds a piece.

Monster - Right. I'll have a piece of the black one and a piece of the tabby !

What football team do vampires support ?

Fangchester United !

What did the witch say to her cat ?

You look familiar !

Why does Dracula like old fashioned things ?

He's never liked anything new fangled !

What is Dracula's favourite TV game show ?

Countdown !

What did the stupid monster buy
when the joke shop ran out
of itching powder ?

A scratch card !

What did the doctor say to the ghost ?

Sorry, but I can't see you at the moment !

Why do cricketers carry garlic
when they are on tour ?

To keep away vampire bats !

Name another of James Bond's
spooky enemies ?

Doctor Nnnnnnnooooooooooo !

Did you hear about the vampire
builder who starved to death ?

He couldn't get blood out of a stone !

What is that ghost doing in the January sales ?

Bargain haunting !

What do you do to keep ghosts fit ?

Run faster !

In the old days ghosts had to take exams before they were allowed to go haunting. They had to have Ooohhh levels !

What was the ghost put in jail for ?

Driving without due scare and attention !

A monster arrived at his friend's house with a skeleton in a bag...

....he said "I've got a bone to pick with you !"

Why was the vampire asked to leave the orchestra ?

His bite was even worse than his Bach !

Why did Frankenstein's monster like
stand up comedians ?

Because they kept him in stitches !

Which Shakespeare play is about
vampires in Scotland ?

Drac-beth !

What do you do with a blue monster ?

Try and cheer him up a bit !

A monster went to his doctor
with acid indigestion...

**"It's no good", said his doctor, "you will just
have to stop drinking acid !"**

Fishy Foolishness...

Which fish runs the undersea mafia?

The Codfather!

Why are Herrings such healthy fish ?

**Because you never see them ill,
only cured !**

★

What do you call a fish that's always asleep ?

A kipper !

★

*Roses are red,
violets are blue,
you look like a
trout, and you
smell like one too !*

★

*If you use a skunk to catch fish you always
catch them hook, line and stinker !*

★

What do you get in a takeaway next to a
power station ?

Nuclear fission chips !

What do dolphins do when they are late ?

They put their skates on !

Where do dolphins learn ?

In Schools, of course !

Where do baby fish go ?

To Plaice-school !

What would you eat in an sunken
pirate ship take away ?

Pizzas of eight !

How do fish go on holiday ?

They take the whale-way !

Which sea creatures never go to parties in
case they are eaten by mistake ?

Jelly fish !

What do you call a naughty little fish ?

Minnow the minx !

Knock, knock...
Who's there ?
Plaice...
Plaice who ?
**Plaice let me in,
I'm wet through !**

Why was the beach wet ?

Because the sea weed !

Why are some shellfish
always bad tempered ?

**They can't help it -
they were
born crabby !**

Where do fish like going for their holidays ?

Finland !

How do fish know exactly
what everything weighs ?

**They always have a set
of scales on them !**

What do sharks eat
at parties ?

**Fish-cakes
Jelly-fish
and
Sandwiches**

Where do whales get
weighed ?

**At a whale - weigh
station !**

What do fish drink ?

**Water of course, they can't use bottle
openers !**

What do fish use to
stop getting
sunburned ?

Sun tan ocean !

166

What sort of paintings do
fish prefer ?

Watercolours !

Who are the worst criminals
in the lake ?

River bank robbers !

What jewellry do lady fish
wear ?

Eel-rings !

Which is the strongest sea
creature ?

The muscle !

Who does all the woodwork in the sea ?

Plankton !

How do fish pass the long winter evenings ?

They tell each other tails !

What did the sea say to the beach ?

It didn't say anything - it waved !

Where do fish keep their savings ?

In the river bank !

What do you call a whale in the Sahara desert ?

Lost !

Which part of the fish do we eat that it doesn't actually have ?

Fish fingers !

Where would you find a pilot whale ?

On board a flying fish !

★

Two men were walking along in the desert. One said to the other "This is a lovely sandy beach." The other replied "Yes, but the tide is a heck of a long way out !"

"Goody," said a shark as a surfer sped by on the crest of a wave, "I love fast food!"

Did you know that fish mums and dads teach their children not to start eating maggots - in case they get hooked!

Why don't fish play tennis?

Because they always get caught up in the net!

What toys do baby fish play with?

Doll - fins!

What fish can make your feet light up?

An electric eel!

What do fish do for adventure ?

They scale mountains !

What sort of fish go to heaven when they die ?

Angel fish !

How do vampire fish communicate ?

With wails !

Roses are red,
violets are pink,
there's an octopus in the bath,
so I'll get washed in the sink !

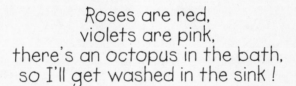

Why do you suck your maggots before putting them on the hook ?

So I can wait for the fish with baited breath !

What do you give a deaf fish ?

A herring aid !

What do fish do when the TV breaks down ?

Send for the electric eel !

Which sea creatures do you need for a game of chess ?

Prawns !

Which fish like to dance in long lines ?

Conga eels !

What do sharks eat for tea ?

Fishermans fingers and chips !

What do chip
shops on other
planets sell?

**Fish and
computer chips!**

★

What do fish parents give their
children at Easter?

Oyster eggs!

★

Hey, Cod, you couldn't loan me
a fiver could you?

**What about the twenty squid
you already owe me?!**

★

Knock, knock...
Who's there?
Kipper...
Kipper who?
**Kipper your mouth shut,
I don't
want anyone to know
I'm here!**

★

What sort of fish
never have any money ?

Poor - poises !

★

What sort of music do
dolphins prefer ?

Sole music !

★

What sort of fish can you train to fetch your
paper every morning ?

A Dogfish !

★

What sort of fish like to
work fingers to
the bone ?

Piranha Fish !

★

What do sharks call people who fall off speedboats ?

Fast food !

Why don't sharks eat people in submarines ?

They don't like tinned food !

Why are fishmongers so unpleasant ?

Because their job makes them sell fish !

What is the best way to get a message to a fish ?

Drop it a line !

Where do fish go for their holidays ?

The Lake District !

Who was the most notorious cowboy fish ?

Billy the Squid !

Why are fish frightened of maths teachers ?

Because they are good anglers !

Why was the kipper sent to jail ?

Because he was gill - ty !

How do fish like their crisps ?

Ready sea salted !

What do fish watch on TV?

One foot in the wave!

Where do fish sleep?

On a sea bed!

What sort of trout can you see after a thunderstorm?

A rainbow!

What did the Eskimo sing at suppertime?

" Whale Meat Again..."

★

What did the *mum* whale say to the cry-baby whale?

Stop blubbering!

What do sharks suck
when they have a
sore throat ?

A Fisherman's Friend !

What game do young
fish play at parties ?

Sardines !

What do fish watch on TV ?

Cod roe nation street !

What sort of fish is always getting
under your feet ?

An eel !

What do you give to a deaf sea nymph ?

A mermaid !

Batty Brain Teasers...

What do gnomes use to get to France?

Cross channel fairies!

What did the space monster say after it had eaten a planet ?

"A Mars a day helps you work, rest and play !"

What is the name of the detective who solves all his crimes by pure accident ?

Sheer - Luck Holmes !

What is the one thing you can catch with your hands tied ?

A cold !

What sort of curry do clock makers eat ?

Tikka !

Why are dentists so miserable ?

Because they are always looking down in the mouth !

Why are men with beards more honest ?

Because they can't tell bare-faced lies !

What do you get if you drop a
piano down a coal mine ?

A flat minor !

What time is it when a Chinese man
visits the dentist ?

Tooth hurty !

Which is the strongest thing in the garden ?

The muscle sprout !

And which is the weakest ?

The weeds !

Why couldn't the squirrel finish his Meccano model of the Forth Bridge ?

Because he'd eaten all the nuts !

We call our dog blacksmith...

...because he sometimes makes a bolt for the back door !

Where did the colonel keep his armies ?

Up his sleevies !

LEFT
RIGHT
LEFT
RIGHT
ATTEN-SHUN

Where would you find a rubber trumpet ?

In an elastic band !

Where does tea
come from ?

**In between the letters
S and U !**

What starts at the
bottom and goes all the
way down to the floor ?

Your leg !

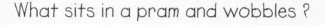

What sits in a pram and wobbles ?

A jelly baby !

How do you start a teddy bear race ?

Ready, Teddy, Go !

How do you make Scotch eggs ?

Feed your chickens whisky !

★

What gets bigger the more you take out of it ?

A hole !

★

How do you make a Swiss roll ?

Push him down an alp !

★

Little dog,
crossing street,
motor car,
sausage meat !

What sort of music was invented by cave men ?

Rock music !

What happened to the man who stole
a lorry load of prunes ?

He was on the run for months !

Waiter, there's a fly in my soup !

**Thank you for telling me, sir,
I'd forgotten to put that
on the bill !**

How do you get rid of a boomerang ?

Throw it down a one-way street !

What's black and white and red all over ?

A newspaper !

How does the snow queen travel about ?

By icicle !

How do you get down from a giraffe ?

You don't get down from a giraffe - you get
down from a duck !

What goes zzub, zzub ?

A bee flying backwards !

Why do cows moo ?

Because their horns don't work !

What is
Dracula's
favourite
TV game show ?

The Crypt-on
factor !

How do you make a
Venetian blind ?

Poke him in the eyes !

What kind of nuts do
the Russians and
Americans send into
space ?

Astronuts !

What sort of music do
miners like to listen to ?

Rock and coal !

*Mary had a little lamb,
it's fleece was black as soot,
and everywhere that Mary went,
its sooty foot it put !*

What do they call the back entrance to a cafeteria ?

The bacteria !

★

What do you call the room where Eskimos train their dogs ?

The mushroom !

★

Who swings from cake to cake ?

Tarzipan !

★

Why did the doll blush ?

Because she saw the teddy bare !

★

How do you know when it's been raining cats and dogs ?

There are lots of little poodles on the pavement !

What do you call a cat with 8 legs ?

An octopus !

What do Eskimos eat for breakfast ?

Ice Crispies !

Where would you find a dog with 4 broken legs ?

Wherever you left it !

Why do potatoes always know what you've done ?

Because they have eyes !

How do carpenters go on holiday ?

They fly there by plane !

★

Jim - Most Egyptian kings were buried with a namafor !

Joe - What's a namafor ?

Jim - Knocking nails in !

★

What do you call someone who puts bulls to sleep ?

A bulldozer !

★

What do you call someone with jelly, cream and fruit in their ears ?

A trifle deaf !

What happened to the cat that swallowed some knitting ?

It had mittens !

What is the most useful cat if you're looking for something ?

A catalogue !

What do you call a cat that knowshow to phone for an ambulance ?

A first aid kit !

Why is using a telephone difficult in China ?

Because there are so many Wings and so many Wongs, you might wing the wong number !

Why did the man order alphabet soup ?

He wanted to eat his words !

Who invented the steam engine ?

No he didn't, it was Watt !

What grows down as it grows up ?

A goose !

Which bird can lift heavy weights ?

A crane !

What's the difference between a butcher and a night watchman?

One weighs a steak, the other stays awake!

How do you stop an elephant stampede?

Telephone the operator and ask to make a reverse charge call!

How many days of the week begin with T?

All except Sunday, when I have coffee!

Where does Dracula stay when he's on holiday in America?

The Vampire State Building!

What's the best thing
to put into a pie ?

Your knife and fork !

Why are teddies good
at being spies ?

Because they can tell bear faced lies !

Where did Noah keep all the elderly bees ?

In his Ark-hives !

Why did the
orchestra have such
bad manners ?

**They didn't know
how to
conduct themselves !**

Good morning Mr
Butcher, do you have a
sheep's head?

No - It's just the way I
part my hair!

Caveman chasing dinosaurs
wants to make a bronto burger
hungry T Rex joins in too...
...hope he enjoyed his human stew!

What do you call someone who is always
working overtime?

A clock mender!

Good morning sir, can
I interest you in a
pocket calculator?

No, thanks, I already
know how many
pockets I've got!

Waiter, there's a fly in my soup !

Don't worry, I'll give you a reduction for the soup he eats !

Why do mum and dad kangaroos hate rainy days ?

Because the children have to play indoors when it rains !

Why do elephants wear green jackets ?

So they can walk across a pool table without being seen !

What's purple and plugs into your TV set ?

An electric plum !

What is yellow and costs a million pounds ?

A banana - I lied about it costing a million pounds !

Why do vampires use more toothpaste than ordinary people?

They have bat breath!

What happens when a frog breaks down?

He gets toad away!

What is green and goes round and round?

An alien in a washing machine!

★

Where was the American declaration of Independence signed?

At the bottom!

PLEASE SIGN HERE ...

Why do bees buzz ?

Because they don't know how to whistle !

★

Why did the stupid
robber carry
two bricks ?

Because the
jewellers shop had
double glazing !

★

My friend is so thin that when
we go to the park
the ducks throw bread at him !

★

Why did the jogger
need so many hankies ?

Because his nose was
always running !

★

What animal uses a nutcracker ?

A squirrel with no teeth !

Why was the football
pitch soggy ?

**Because the
players were
always dribbling !**

What do you give to
injured fruit ?

Lemonade !

What is all that rubbish in the restaurant ?

Oh, someone left a tip !

What do chiropodists eat for breakfast ?

Corn flakes !

What do cats eat for breakfast ?

Shredded tweet !

What is the difference between a march hare and a six pound note ?

One is a mad bunny, the other's bad money !

The police are looking for a burglar with a wooden leg called Blenkinsop...

...What's his other leg called ?

★

Jane - My boyfriend reminds me of the sea !

Joe - You mean he's strong, exciting and full of surprises ?

Jane - No, he makes me sick !

★

What do you call the machine the butcher uses to write out his orders ?

A tripewriter !

Medical Mayhem...

Doctor, doctor, I think I'm invisible !

Who said that ?

Doctor, doctor, I think I'm a pair of curtains !

Pull yourself together !

Doctor, doctor, my wife thinks
she's a motorbike !

Give her two of these pills and she'll be cured !

But how will I get home then ?

Doctor, doctor, I have an inferiority complex !

Hmm. Not a very big one is it !

Doctor, doctor, I'm shrinking !

Well, you'll just have to be a little patient !

Doctor, doctor, my wife thinks she's a chicken!

Do you want me to cure her?

No, I just wondered if you had any good egg recipes!

Doctor, doctor, everyone keeps ignoring me!

Next patient please!

Doctor, doctor, I think I'm a pack of cards!

You'll just have to deal with it yourself!

Doctor, doctor, I think I'm a mousetrap!

Snap out of it!

Doctor, doctor, all my friends think I'm a liar !

I find that hard to believe !

Doctor, doctor, I keep thinking that my parents are goats !

When did you start to have these thoughts ?

When I was a kid !

I SENT HIM HOME TO FETCH HIS NANNY!

Doctor, doctor, I think I'm becoming invisible !

I'm sorry, I can't see you now !

Doctor, doctor, I can't seem to get to sleep at night !

Sleep on the windowsill, you'll soon drop off !

Doctor, doctor, I have a lot of wind, can you give me anything for it?

Certainly, here's a kite!

★

Doctor, doctor, my hair is falling out, have you anything to keep it in?

Try this paper bag!

★

Doctor, doctor, you know those pills you gave me for a headache - well they worked. Now can you give me something to take the headache away!

★

Doctor, doctor, I think I'm a billiard ball!

Sorry, you'll have to go to the end of the cue!

Doctor, doctor, I keep thinking I'm a roll of film !

Don't worry, I'm sure nothing will develop !

★

Nurse, nurse, I need to see a doctor !

Which doctor?

No, just an ordinary one !

★

HE'S PAYING !

Doctor, doctor, I think I have a split personality !

In that case I will have to charge you double !

★

Doctor, doctor, I'm a little hoarse !

I'll be with you in a minute - just take your saddle off and relax !

Doctor, doctor, I swallowed a spoon !

Just sit there quietly and don't stir !

Doctor, doctor, I've lost my memory !

That's terrible. When did you first notice ?

When did I notice what ?

Doctor, doctor, I think I'm a dog !

Well, fetch this stick then roll over and let me tickle your tummy !

Will that cure me ?

No, but I was never allowed to have a pet as a child !

Doctor, doctor, I think I have a split personality !

I'm sorry, one of you will have to wait outside !

Doctor, doctor, my wife wants to know if you can stop me being so argumentative ?

I'm sorry Mr. Brown, there's nothing I can do !

Yes there is !

I'm not feeling myself today, so can you ask the doctor to call round and see Mr. Smith instead !

Doctor, doctor, I keep thinking that I have been here before !

Oh. It's you again !

Doctor, doctor, can you help me to stop smoking ?

Well, you could try not setting fire to your trousers !

Doctor, doctor, can you give me a sick note to get a week off school ?

You look perfectly healthy to me !

Yes, but I'm sick of going to school !

Doctor, doctor, I've just swallowed a tin of gloss paint !

Yes, my receptionist said you'd taken a shine to her !

Doctor, doctor my wife just buried my radio in the garden !

Why did she do that ?

The batteries were dead !

Doctor, doctor, I've got athlete's foot in my head !

What makes you think that ?

Because my nose keeps running !

Doctor, doctor, what's
the best cure for
water on the knee ?

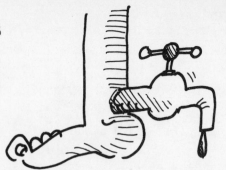

A tap on the ankle !

Doctor, doctor, I have flowers growing out of
the top of my head !

Don't worry, it's just a beauty spot !

Doctor, doctor, I think I need glasses !

I'll say you do - this is a fish and chip shop !

Doctor, doctor, I'm suffering from delusions
of grandeur !

Sit down, your Majesty, and tell me all about it !

Doctor, doctor, how can I lose 15 kilos
of ugly fat ?

How about cutting your head off ?

Doctor, doctor, I'm covered in spots - I need to do something about it straight away !

Now, now, let's not do anything rash !

Doctor, doctor, my dog has just bitten me !

In that case we will need to check for infection !

Thank you - that will put my mind at rest !

So, when can you bring the dog in?

Doctor, doctor, I kissed a girl and she turned into a frog !

Where is she now ?

Waiting in the croakroom !

Doctor, doctor, I've swallowed my pen, what should I do ?

You'll have to use a pencil !

Doctor, doctor I can't stop sneezing - what can you give me ?

A tissue ?

Oh, no, it's happening to you as well now !

Doctor, doctor, I'm worried. This is the first time I've had an operation !

I know how you feel - it's the first time I've done one !

Doctor, doctor, I get so nervous when I drive I keep bumping into things !

Don't worry I'll prescribe a crash course !

Doctor, doctor I've gone blind, what should I do ?

Put your crash helmet on the right way round !

Doctor, doctor, I've got my foot caught in a colander !

Hmm. Sounds like a strained ankle !

Doctor, doctor, there's a man at the surgery door with a wooden leg !

Tell him to hop it !

Doctor, doctor, the chemist says these pills you prescribed me are for cows !

Well, you said you wanted to be as strong as an ox !

Doctor, doctor, I keep seeing numbers in front of my eyes all the time !

Take two of these pills every night !

Will I ever be cured ?

I wouldn't count on it !

Doctor, doctor, I keep seeing spots
in front of my eyes !

Have you seen an optician !

No, just the spots !

Doctor, doctor, there's a rumour going round
that you're a vampire !

Nonsense ! Necks please !

Doctor, doctor, I keep stealing things from
electrical shops !

**Take these pills twice a day, and if they don't
work bring me a CD player next time you come !**

Doctor, doctor, wherever I
go I hear this ringing
in my ears !

**I'm not surprised, you
always wear
bell bottoms !**

Doctor, doctor, I think I'm a pack of cards !

You'll just have to play patient for a while !

Doctor, doctor, why are you
so short tempered ?

I don't have enough patients !

Doctor, doctor, three beer kegs have
just fallen on me ?

Don't worry, it was light ale !

Doctor, doctor, I think I'm turning
into a mummy !

Hmmm, better keep well wrapped up !

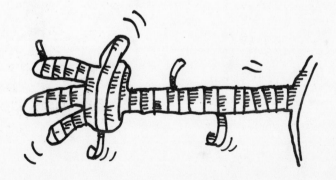

Doctor, doctor, I think I need some antibiotics !

Why, are you feeling ill ?

No, but my auntie feels terrible !

★

Doctor, doctor, I think I've caught a computer virus !

I've warned you before about eating chips !

★

Doctor, doctor, how can I get rid of my fat belly ?

Have you tried to diet ?

Yes, but whatever colour I use it still looks too big !

★

Doctor, doctor, I have
these little flowers
growing out of my feet !

**It's all right, they're
just corn flowers !**

Doctor, doctor, my husband has gone all furry,
and he smells of mints all the time !

**This could be serious, sounds like he's turning
into a polo bear !**

Doctor, doctor, I've lost my memory !

**Well, Mr Smith, if you would like to pay the
outstanding £10,000 from your last bill
I'll have a look at you !**

Ah, Mr. Smith, did you drink your medicine after
your bath like I asked you to ?

**No doctor, after I had drunk the bath I had no
room for the medicine !**

Nurse, nurse, will the doctor be around soon ?

No, he'll be tall and slim as usual !

Doctor, doctor, after the operation will I be able to play the piano ?

Of course Mr Blenkinsop !

That's brilliant - because I can't now !

Doctor, doctor, I'm insomniac !

Don't worry, we treat everyone regardless of their religion !

Doctor, doctor, I'm scared, this is my first operation !

Yeah ! Me too !

Doctor, doctor, my husband keeps dressing
up like a French soldier !

Another case of legionnaires disease !

Doctor, doctor, I need you to recommend
a good plastic surgeon !

Why, what do you need done ?

**Well, I put the TV too close to the fire
and it's melted !**

Doctor, doctor, I've started having dizzy spells !

When do they start ?

Whenever I step off the roundabout !

Doctor, doctor, I just know that you can help
me with my flat feet !

What do you want me to do ?

**Just reverse your car off them and they
would be a lot better !**

Doctor, doctor, I'm suffering
from terrible insomnia !

Oh! I'm sure all you need is a
good night's sleep !

Doctor, doctor, can you help
me to lose weight ?

Well, you could lose 20 kilos straight away !

How on earth do I do that ?

Put down those shopping bags !

Doctor, doctor, I've just swallowed 70 pence ?

Why on earth did you
do that !

I was feeling ill, and I
thought the change
would do me good !

Doctor, doctor, what is good for a headache ?

**Banging your head against
a wall works every time !**

Doctor, doctor, I've just been bitten by a snake
- do you think there is any chance
of an infection ?

**I wouldn't have thought so, snakes are
pretty resilient creatures !**

Doctor, doctor, my snoring is
driving my neighbours crazy !

**Well, maybe you should sleep in
your own home from now on !**

Doctor, doctor, my pig has pimples,
what should I give him ?

Try this oinkment !

Doctor, doctor, I
only have one
tooth, what
should I do ?

**You'll just have to
grin and bare it !**

Doctor, doctor, my family think I'm crazy !

Why on earth do they think that !

Because I like pork pies !

But I like pork pies too !

Then you'll have to come round and see my collection, I've got thousands of them !

Crazy Crosses...

What do you get if you cross your mum's sister with an Eskimo?

Auntie freeze!

What do you get if
you cross a
kangaroo with a
sheep?

A woolly jumper!

What do you get if you cross a kangaroo with
a line of people waiting for a bus?

A queue jumper!

What do you get if you cross a road
without looking?

Knocked down, stupid!

What do you get if you cross a
policeman with a landscape artist?

A constable!

What do you get if you cross a fish with
a children's' nanny?

Mrs. Troutfire!

What do you get if you cross an
elephant with a mouse ?

Ten foot holes in your skirting board !

What do you get
if you cross
a bear with a
cow pat ?

Winnie the Pooh !

What do you get if you cross a chicken with a
skunk ?

A fowl smell !

What do you get if you cross a fly
with a detective ?

A police insector !

What do you get if you cross a pair of
wellingtons with a packet of jelly babies ?

Very chewy, waterproof sweets !

What do you get if you cross a pig
with an ambulance ?

A Hambulance !

What do you get if you cross
a window cleaner with a giraffe ?

A window cleaner who doesn't
need any ladders
!

What do you get
if you cross
a pig
with Dracula ?

A Hampire !

What do you get if you cross a chicken
with someone who tells jokes ?

A comedihen !

or

Lenny Henry !

What do you get if you cross a cricketer
with a hat ?

Two bowlers !

What do you get if you
cross a football team with
ice cream ?

Aston Vanilla !

What do you get if you
cross
hockey equipment with
hiking gear ?

A pucksack !

What do you get if you cross a pig with a
mathematical quantity ?

A pork pi !

What do you get if you cross a goldfish
bowl with a TV ?

Tele-fish-ion !

What do you get if you cross an explorer
with a cat ?

Christopher Columpuss !

What do you get if
you cross a
cowboy with
a dinosaur ?

Tyrannosaurus Tex !

What do you get if you cross a pudding
with an ape ?

Lemon meringue-utan pie !

What do you get if you cross the mafia
and a box of teaspoons ?

A gangstir !

What do you get if you cross a river with a broken bridge ?

Very wet I should think !

★

What do you get if you cross a tree with a fruit ?

A Pineapple !

★

What do you get if you cross a maths teacher with anything ?

A maths teacher !

★

Now... TURN TO PAGE 46 OF YOUR HARD MATHS BOOK !

What do you get if you cross a pony with a TV detective ?

Inspector Horse !

★

What do you get if you cross a famous detective and a lot of good fortune ?

Sheer luck Holmes !

What do you get if you cross a
cow pat and a microprocessor ?

A com-pooh-ter !

What do you get if you cross a mouse
and an elephant ?

An animal that's scared to look in the mirror !

What do you get if
you cross a dog
with someone
worried about
something ?

Nervous Rex !

What do you get if you cross a duck and
a TV programme ?

A Duckumentary !

What do you get if you cross garden birds
with a famous aerobatic display team ?

The Red Sparrows !

What do you get if you cross two rows of
cabbages with a main road?

A dual cabbageway !

What do you get if you
cross kitchen
equipment with a
vampire ?

Count spatula !

What do you get if you
cross a giant ape with
an aeroplane ?

King Kongcorde !

What do you get if you cross a farm worker with some cheese and pickle ?

A ploughman's lunch !

What do you get if you cross a cat and an octopus ?

A cat-o-nine-tails !

What do you get if you cross a pop group with a ton of latex ?

A rubber band !

What do you get if you cross a cow pat with a boomerang ?

A nasty smell you can't get rid of !

★

What do you get if you cross dandruff
and a French fried potato ?

A chip on your shoulder !

What do you get if you cross a
stick of dynamite and a pig ?

Bangers !

What do you get if you
cross a giraffe
and a cow ?

**Something you need a
ladder to milk !**

What do you get if you
cross a
traffic warden
with a dog ?

A barking ticket !

What do you get if you cross a coal mine
with a cow ?

A pit - bull !

What do you get if you cross a cow with
a CD player ?

Pop - Moosic !

What do you get if you mislay your violin
in a match factory ?

Fiddlesticks !

What do you get if you cross a fox
with a carrot ?

**Something that no rabbit will dare to steal
from the vegetable patch !**

What do you get if you put a car engine into
an old sailing ship ?

About 45 miles to the galleon !

What do you get if you cross a pantomime
actor with an opera singer ?

The panto of the opera !

Oh, no you don't...

Oh, yes you do...

Oh, no you don't...

What do you get if you
cross a box of hankies
with a cold ?

A - A - A -tishoo !

What do you get if you
cross a glove puppet
with a mouse ?

Sooty and squeak !

What game do you get if you cross
frogs legs and whisky ?

Hop scotch !

What do you get if you cross a scary
story and a dog ?

Someone who is terrier - fied !

★

What do you get if you cross a ghost
and a garden party ?

A fete worse than death !

★

What do you get if you
cross a football team
and a pig ?

Queens Pork Rangers !

★

What do you get if you
cross the X files with
something you keep
your fuel in ?

A coal Scully !

★

What do you get if you cross a window with a guillotine ?

A pane in the neck !

What do you get if
you cross a
carrier pigeon and
a woodpecker ?

**A bird that
knocks before
delivering the
message !**

What do you get if you cross a
cow with a thief ?

A beef burglar !

What do you get if you cross a pig with an
expensive car ?

A sausage roller !

What do you get if you cross the Radio Times
with a microchip ?

Lots of computer programmes on TV !

What do you get if you cross a heavy goods
vehicle and an ice cream ?

An articulated lolly !

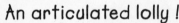

What do you get if you cross a film director
and a horse drawn vehicle ?

Orson Kart !

What do you get if you cross a James Bond
movie and a footballer ?

Goal - finger !

What do you get if you
cross a spy and a duvet ?

An under-cover agent !

What do you get if you
cross a ghost
and an optician ?

Spook - tacles !

What do you get if you cross a giant
monopoly set with a safari guide ?

A big game hunter !

What do you get if
you cross a man
inside your TV set and
someone very brainy ?

In - tele - gent !

What do you get
when teenage aliens
have a party?

A space racket!

What do you get if
you cross a
policeman and a tree?

Special Branch!

What do you get if you cross a
vampire and a boat?

A blood vessel!

What do you get if
you draw dots
and dashes on
your hanky?

A code in the nose!

What do you get if you cross a spot, a man
who saved people
from the guillotine and a tin of red paint ?

The Scarlet Pimple !

What do you get
if you cross a dog
with a tree ?

**Something with
a completely
silent bark !**

What do you get if you cross a French and a
German fortune telling device ?

A oui - ja board !

What do you get if you cross a TV detective
and Darth Vader ?

Inspector Force !

What do you get if you cross
a field with some cows in it ?

A pat on the shoe !

What do you get if you
cross a postman, cow dung,
a tap on the head and a
small piece of butter, and
the whole thing sounds like
an outboard engine... ?

Pat, pat, pat, pat...!

What do get when you
cross an angry young man
and someone who can't
decide which of
his 20 shoes to wear ?

A ten-pair tantrum !

What do you get if
you cross a cow
and a moped ?

A mooter scooter !

What do you get if
you cross cats and
dogs and put
them in cars ?

Datsun cogs !

★

What do you get if you cross
a painting and a rodent ?

A mouse - terpiece !

★

What do you get if you cross the African
jungle with a map of Manchester ?

Completely lost !

★

What do you get if
you cross a
portable stereo
and a pig ?

A Porkman !

★

What do you get if you cross a
footballer with a ghost ?

A Ghoulkeeper !

What do you get if you cross an
angry rabbit and an oven ?

A hot-cross bun !

What do you get if you cross
a dog with a scientist ?

Something in a lab coat !

What do you get if you
cross a party game with
a herd of cows ?

Moosical chairs !

What do you get if you
cross two vampire
Red Indians ?

Blood brothers !

Holiday Howlers...

Our maths teacher is going
to the Bahamas this *Summer* !

Jamaica ?

No, she wanted to go !

When we went on holiday last year - the
aeroplane was so old...

...it had solid tyres !

*...the two previous owners were the
Wright Brothers !*

...one of the seats said "Reserved for
Julius Caesar" !

*...the co-pilot had to keep running to the
tail to rewind the motor !*

...the seats were covered in
dinosaur hide !

*...the pilot was taught to fly by
Baron Von Richtofen !*

Who always gets the sack on his first
day at work ?

Father Christmas !

Dear Santa...

If I'm good
it's understood
that you'll bring me
a new CD.

If I'm kind
I know I'll find
a guitar to play
on Christmas Day.

So from now on,
You're going to find,
that I'll be helpful,
good and kind,
and I intend to stay
that way !
At least, that is, till
Boxing day !

Where do Santa's workers go when they
are sick ?

The National Elf Service !

What do you call two girls with Christmas decorations on their heads ?

Holly and Ivy !

★

Where do snowmen go to dance ?

Snowballs !

What do you call someone who casts spells at the seaside ?

A Sandwitch !

Two elephants wanted to go swimming at the seaside but they couldn't - they only had one pair of trunks between them !

What do you call a man with a bucket and spade on his head ?

Doug !

We stayed in a really posh hotel on our holiday last year - it was so posh that the number for room service was ex-directory!

Waiter! This egg is bad!

That's not my fault. I only laid the table!

How does a vampire cross the channel to France?

In a blood vessel!

How do fish go on holiday?

By octobus!

What sort of clothes do people wear
in very hot countries ?

Blazers !

Where are the Andes ?

On the ends of your armies !

Why do birds fly South in the Winter ?

It's too far to walk !

When bees go on holiday where do
they wait for the coach ?

At a buzz stop !

What is grey, has four legs and a trunk ?

A mouse going on holiday !

Why did the elephant wear sunglasses on the beach ?

Because he didn't want to be recognised !

A witch wanted to go on a motor cycling holiday...

...so she bought a brrooommm stick !

"Good morning ladies and gentlemen. Welcome aboard the World's first ever fully computerised aeroplane. There is no need for a pilot or co-pilot on this aircraft, as everything is fully automated. We are currently flying at 30,000 feet and everything is working perfectly...working porfectly...burking lurfectly...smirking carpetly..."

What flavour crisps can you use to take you on holiday ?

Plane !

Where do school dinner ladies go on holiday ?

Greece !

Why do policemen like to go to
discos when they are on holiday ?

They really enjoy the beat !

What's big and grey and flies you to
your holiday destination ?

A jumbo jet !

*Three friends went on a cruise holiday, but
were shipwrecked on a desert island. A good
fairy came and gave them one wish each. The
first two men wished they were back at home
with their families. The third man thought for
a minute and said, "It's quiet around here all
on my own, I wish my two friends were still
here with me !"*

Did you hear about the elephant who couldn't
go on holiday - the notice said that all cases,
bags and trunks had to go through the
airport X-Ray machine !

Waiter - do you have frog's legs ?

Yes, monsieur !

Well, hop into the kitchen and get me a steak !

Tourist-Do you have a room for the night ?

Hotelier-Certainly, sir. £40 a night or £10 a night if you make your own bed.

Tourist - I'll take the £10 room please !

Hotelier - Fine. You'll find the wood in the room and I'll bring the hammer and nails up in a minute !

What do jelly babies travel in on holiday ?

A jelly copter !

Where do monks go for a break ?

Holy-day camps !

Two friends had enjoyed a great days
fishing on a lake.

*"We must come here again," said one,
"but how will we ever find this same spot
on such a huge lake ?"*

**"No problem," said his friend, "I've marked
an X on the side of the boat !"**

What do cavemen do on holiday ?

They go out night-clubbing !

HOW DO CAVEMEN
AFFORD HOLIDAYS ?

They club together !

Did you remember to bring the
sun-protection cream ?!

Yes, but I would have thought the sun would
be used to the heat by now !

★

Passenger - I'm
nervous, I've never
flown before ?

Hostess - Oh, don't you
start, I've got enough
trouble with the pilot !

★

My holiday was in ruins this year !

I'm sorry to hear that !

Oh! it's OK - I went on an archaeological dig !

Dear Santa...

I've been good - really means -
- I haven't broken any
windows for a whole
week now !

I'm kind to dumb animals - really means - I
**sometimes help my little brother with
his homework !**

I help old ladies to cross the road - really
means - **I dropped a bottle of cooking oil
outside the old folks' home and they all
skidded on it !**

I stay behind at school all the time to do extra
work - really means -
I am constantly in detention !

I look forward to receiving a little something
from you in my Christmas stocking - really
means - **Fill up the two duvet covers and three
pillow cases with presents fat man or there'll
be trouble !!**

★

What did the Martian
bring home from his holiday in outer space ?

Sticks of rocket !

What do movie directors put on their
Christmas cakes ?

Starzipan !

Why are you eating all those
tins of baked beans ?

**I'm going windsurfing this
afternoon !**

Where does a vampire go to see
the illuminations ?

Dracpool !

What do you call a reggae singer who
looks after chairs on the beach ?

Desmond Deckchair !

How did you find your steak sir ?

**Easy, I just moved these two chips
and there it was !**

Where does a monster sleep on a
camping holiday ?

In a sleeping bog !

Which holiday camp do vampires prefer ?

Batlins !

What do people wear on their heads
in very cold countries ?

Ice caps !

Where do jockeys spend their holidays ?

Horse - tria !

Where do birds go for a holiday ?

Coven - tree !

How do fish go on holiday ?

By British Whale !

What is grey, has four legs and two trunks?

An elephant going on holiday!

Why did the cow use sun tan oil?

Because she didn't want to tan her hide!

Why did the witch go
to France?

**Because she fancied a
spell abroad!**

How do footballers go on holiday?

By coach!

How do cavemen get to their holiday
destinations?

They fly club class!

Why do monsters put people in their suitcases ?

They like to take a packed lunch !

What do monsters like to eat best on holiday ?

Beaches and cream !

Where do you go to see the world's untidiest monster ?

Loch Mess !

★

Tourist - Can I have breakfast in bed ?

Hotelier - Of course, but most of our guests find a plate more sensible ?!

Mirthful
Miscellany...

Did you hear about the girl who
fell asleep with her head
under the pillow...

...the fairies came and
took out all her teeth!

Where has all the lemonade gone. I though we agreed to have half the bottle each?

We did - my half was the bottom half, and I had to drink yours to get to it !

Fish and chips and mushy peas ? But I ordered a ploughman's lunch !

That's what then ploughman is having for his lunch today !

Doctor, doctor, my little boy has swallowed all the coins from my purse !

Don't worry - the change will probably do him good !

Dad, am I worth a million pounds to you ?

Of course you are, son !

In that case can you lend me £10 of it now, I want to go to the cinema !

What is a vampire's favourite pudding ?

Clotted Dick !

What do you get if you dial 666 ?

Three policemen standing on their heads !

Where does the local policeman live ?

At 999, Letsby Avenue !

Why was the policeman offered a job
on the buses ?

Because copper is such a good conductor !

What did the burglar say to the blonde
policeman who caught him breaking into
a big top ?

It's a fair cop, fair cop !

Did you hear about the policeman who was invited to join the Royal Shakespeare Company...

...he always gave an arresting performance !

What does a policeman call an overdue library fine ?

An old bill !

What goes ' ello, ello, tick, tock, woof, ello, ello, tick, tock, woof...'

A police watchdog !

What goes 'ho, ho, ho, ho, clonk'

Someone laughing their head off !

Why do witches fly around on broomsticks ?

Because vacuum cleaners don't have long enough flexes !

What do you call a stupid vampire ?
A blood clot !

What did the policeman say to his tummy ?

I've got you under a vest !

What do you do if your nose goes on strike ?

Picket !

What tables can't you eat ?

Vegetables !

Why do bicycles never do anything exciting ?

Because they are always two tyred !

What do you have to know before you can start training a pet ?

More than the pet !

What comes after the letter A ?

The rest of the alphabet !

How do you lift an elephant

Sit him on an acorn and wait for it to grow !

I would tell you the joke about the bed...

...but it hasn't been made up yet !

What is red on the outside and grey
and crowded on the inside ?

A bus full of elephants !

What does an elephant
do when it rains ?

Gets wet !

How do you stop your dog barking in the back of the car ?

Put it in the front !

What is worse than finding a maggot when you bite into an apple ?

Finding half of one !

What is brown and sticky ?

A stick !

What is green and bouncy ?

A spring onion !

Why do wizards drink so much tea ?

Because sorcerers need cuppas !

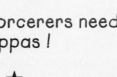

How do you cut through the waves ?

With a sea-saw !

What sort of nuts sneeze the most ?

Cashews !

What exams are horses good at ?

Hay levels !

Why did the owl make everyone laugh ?

Because he was a hoot !

If your cat ate a lemon what would he become ?

A sourpuss !

Will you remember me tomorrow ?

Yes !

Will you remember me next week ?

Yes !

Will you remember me next month ?

Yes !

Will you remember me in a year ?

Yes !

Knock, knock

Who's there ?

You see, you've forgotten me already !

Knock Knock...
Who's there ?
Ivor...
Ivor who ?
Ivor good mind not to
tell you !

What do you give a seasick elephant ?

Plenty of room !

Knock Knock...
Who's there ?
Justin...
Justin who ?
Justin time for a party !

How can you tell if there's an elephant in your school custard ?

It's more lumpy than usual !

What is the difference between a jeweller and a jailor ?

One sells watches the other watches cells !

Which is the strongest day of the week ?

Sunday - because all the others are weak days !

Why didn't the viper viper nose ?

Because the adder adder handkerchief !

What is the difference between a fisherman and an idle schoolboy ?

One baits hooks, the other hates books !

Why did the jam roll ?

Because it saw the apple turnover !

Two cows were talking in a field..

first cow - 'Are you worried about this mad cow disease ?'

second cow - 'Why should I worry about that - I'm a penguin !'

What do you get if you cross a snowman and a mosquito ?

Frostbite !

What zooms along the bed of the lake ?

A motor pike and side carp !

Why shouldn't you complain about
the price of a train ticket ?

Because it's bound to be fare !

How do you tell which end
of a worm is the head ?

**Tickle it in the middle and see
which end laughs !**

Romeo - Do you love me ?

Juliet - Of course I do !

Romeo - Then whisper something
soft and sweet.

Juliet - Lemon Meringue Pie !

I'll teach you to throw stones at my greenhouse !

I wish you would - I keep missing !

Did you hear about the man who was hit on the head with a pan full of curry ?

He ended up in a Korma !

There were two bishops in a bed - which one wore the nightie ?

Mrs. Bishop !

What happens when pigs fly ?

The price of bacon goes up !

Why did the tap dancer have to retire ?

He kept falling into the sink !

What is the difference between a nail
and a bad boxer ?

**One gets knocked in, the other gets
knocked out !**

How many ears has Captain Kirk ?

**Three ! A right ear, a left ear and a
final frontier !**

How does a chimpanzee make toast ?

Puts it under the gorilla !

What do jelly babies
wear in the rain ?

Gum boots !

What is small, green
and goes camping ?

A boy sprout !

What does a Swedish Fred Flintstone shout ?

Abba dabba Doo !

★

What do you get when you cross a jelly with a sheep dog ?

Collie wobbles !

What kind of ears does a train have ?

Engineers !

Why was the farmer hopping mad ?

Because someone trod on his corn !

Joe - One of my ancestors died at Waterloo !

Jim - **Really - which platform ?**

Why is a farmer cruel ?

Because he pulls corn by its ears !

How do you use an Egyptian Mummy's doorbell ?

Toot-and-come-in !

Why couldn't the butterfly get into the dance ?

Because it was a moth-ball !

Why did the orange stop halfway up the hill ?

Because it ran out of juice !

Joe - Mum, do you notice any change in me ?

Mum - No, why do you ask ?

Joe - Because I've just swallowed 5p !

How do you know when there's an elephant hiding under your bed ?

Your nose touches the ceiling !

Waiter, waiter, what do you call this ?

It's bean soup sir !

I don't care what it's been - what is it now ? !

I would tell you the joke about the butter - but you would only spread it !

And - I would tell you the joke about the fence - but I know you would never get over it !

Dracula's School Report

Reading - Good
Writing - Average
Cricket - shows promise as a bat !

What did Tarzan say when he saw the elephants coming over the hill ?

Here come the elephants !

What shoot along the washing line at 70 miles an hour ?

Hondapants !

How can you keep cool at a football match ?

Stand next to a fan !

What do you get if you cross a crocodile with a rose ?

I don't know but I wouldn't try smelling it !

Who did Dracula marry ?

The girl necks door !

*Did you hear about the two flies playing
football in the saucer - they were practising
for the cup !*

What did the baby chicken say when his mum
laid a jar of orange jam ?

Ooh ! Look what marmalade !

Shall I tell you the joke about
the packet of corn flakes ?

I hope you've got plenty of time - It's a cereal !

How do you keep an idiot in suspense ?

I'll tell you tomorrow !

Where do monsters stay on holiday ?

In a bed-for-breakfast hotel !

What is the difference between an African elephant and an Indian elephant ?

African elephants can't cook curry !

What sort of car does a farmer's dog drive ?

A Range Rover !

Did you hear about the burglar who was arrested in his shower - he was trying to make a clean getaway !

How do you make a cake stand ?

Hide all the chairs !

Policeman - You just went through a red light !

Motorist - Sorry, blame it on my good manners. My mum taught me never to look when someone was changing !

And always remember that before you give someone a piece of your mind, make sure you can manage on what you have left !

What sort of shoes can you make from banana skins ?

Slippers !

Jim- My sister married an Irishman !

Joe - Oh, Really ?

Jim - No, O'Reilly !

Woodwork teacher - What are you making ?

Pupil - A portable.

Woodwork teacher - A portable what ?

Pupil - I don't know yet - I only just made the handle !

Mum - Why haven't you changed the water in the goldfish bowl ?

Daughter - Because they haven't drunk the first lot yet !

What do you do with a sick budgie ?

Send it for tweetment !

Your teeth are like stars...

(they come out at night)

Your cheeks are like petals...

(bicycle petals)

What are those little bongos dangling from your ears ?

They're my ear drums !

Did you hear about the man who went to the doctor and told him he thought he was a suitcase ?

The doctor sent him packing !

What do you get if you cross a pig with a flea ?

Pork scratchings !

Which of Tarzan's underwear swing through
the trees ?

Junglepants !

Why is a bull that has swallowed
a hand grenade like a yeti ?

They are both abominable !

Now for some composers...

Which composer can't you find ?

Haydn !

*Which composer can help you with the
shopping ?*

Liszt !

Which composer sounds like a dog ?

Bach !

★

A man walked into a bar. What did he say ?

"OOf !" It was an iron bar !

★

Why is it dangerous to tell jokes when
you're skating ?

Because the ice might crack up !

★

Cannibal One - I don't know what to make of
my children these days ?

Cannibal Two - How about a curry !

What four things contain milk ?

**Butter, cheese, er... a cow
and the lorry from the dairy !**

Where does a vampire keep his money ?

In a bank a - Count !

What is made from fruit, served with custard
and moans all the time you're eating it ?

Apple grumble !

What did the man say when he went in to the
building society to arrange a mortgage and
was served by a masked man ?

I'd like to see the loan arranger, Lone Ranger !

Did you hear about the cabbage whose neighbour won the lottery ?

...he was green with envy !

Where does a monster relax on holiday ?

On a ghoulf course !

Yuck - this lettuce tastes of soap !

Of course it does, I've just washed it !

What happened to the man who discovered electricity ?

He got a nasty shock !

Why do witches keep pet cats ?

Because they like to see a familiar face around the house !

What did the vampire with a cold ask his chemist for ?

Something to stop his coffin !

Cannibal One - Hello dear, I've brought a friend home for dinner !

Cannibal Two - Why didn't you tell me ? I've just cooked a lasagne !

MMmmm! That cake was lovely and warm !

It should be - the cat has been asleep on it all afternoon !

What's that crackling - are you listening to an old radio set ?

No, I'm eating a pork sandwich !

How do you know when a bicycle is angry ?

It has a cross-bar !

Should you cycle to school
on an empty stomach ?

You could, but it would be easier on a bicycle !

What musical device follows a bee ?

C D !

Blenkinsop - why have you brought a fish into
music class ?

**You said we were
going to play
scales today, sir !**

I would tell you the joke about the
highly contagious disease...

...but I'm sure you would get it straight away !

What is green and turns red
at the flick of a switch ?

A frog in a blender !

What game does a vampire play while he's
waiting for his
coffin lid to be delivered ?

Draughts !

Why was the vampire kicked out of school ?

He failed his end of term blood test !

Spock - you've got splinters in your hand !

Yes, I was leafing through the captain's log !

Why did the farmer send his cows to the gym twice a week ?

He wanted low fat milk !

Which insect breathes fire ?

A dragonfly !

Why do wizards have fond memories of school ?

Because they always came top in spelling !

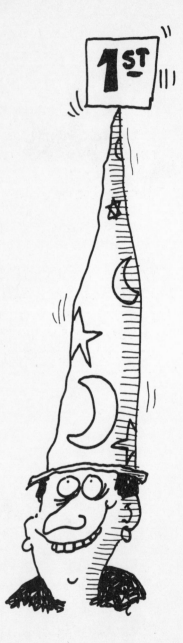

What do you call a vampire's leader ?

A Neckerchief !

What do you give a
vampire for Christmas ?

Blood bath salts !

Why did England lose
their last cricket match ?

**Because they let
the goldfish bowl !**

What do monsters do at the disco ?

Break dancing !

Where do you take a sick bird ?

To the casualty wing !

★

How can you help save a sick vampire ?

Stick your neck out for him !

★

What do you call a
vampire who likes
dipping biscuits
in his blood ?

Count Dunkula !

★

Why did the chewing gum cross the road ?

Because it was stuck to the chicken's foot !

★

Knock Knock...
Who's there ?
Carlos...
Carlos who ?
**Carlos on the phone
and I'll pop round
for tea !**

★

Which part of a computer squeaks ?

The mouse !

What is the difference between someone in a hurry and someone wasteful ?

One makes haste the other makes waste !

What drink grows on trees ?

Leaf tea !

What does a modern Father Christmas deliver presents in ?

A Holly - copter !

Where does a monster keep his school books ?

In his shocker !

★

What sort of films do stupid monsters make ?

Error movies !

★

How do sharks keeps the weeds down in their gardens ?

They use a garden hake !

★

What is the quickest way to fire a monster ?

Ask him to check a dragon's teeth !

★

Mum, I don't like grandad !

Well just leave him on the side of your plate !

★

What do you do if a vampire bites
your bottom ?

I don't know, but I wouldn't recommend turning
the other cheek !

★

Would a vampire be grateful if you
gave him a place to stay ?

Yes, I'm certain he would fang
you for it !

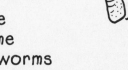

Nobody loves me
everyone hates me
think I'll go and eat worms

I bites off the head
and sucks the juice
and throws the skins away

Nobody loves me
everyone hates me
think I'll go and eat worms

★

Why did the monster eat the coat ?

Someone told him it was a dinner jacket !

What do vampires sing at New Year ?

For the sake of old fang syne !

But Mummy, I don't want to go to China !

Shut up and keep swimming !

Why shouldn't you eat scotch eggs on an empty stomach ?

They will roll off !

What do you tie a piano to the moving van with ?

Chord !

What do robot children do every morning at school ?

They go to assembly !

Why couldn't the robot go to the cinema ?

He hadn't any brass !

★

What can you give a
sickly robot ?

Iron tablets !

What sort of
chocolate do
robots like best ?

Fruit and nut !

I wish I had been born
200 years ago !

Why is that ?

**Because there
wouldn't have been so
much History to learn
at school !**

★

What do you call a skeleton dressed in a kilt ?

Bony Prince Charlie !

Will the band play anything I ask ?

Certainly !

Ask them to play cards !

What kind of ears does a
mountain have ?

Mountaineers !

Are you any good at maths ?

Yes and no !

What do you mean 'Yes and No' ?

Yes, I'm no good at maths !

Joe - If you found £10 would you keep it ?

Jim - No, that would be dishonest!
I'd spend it !!

Why do people employ skeletons ?

Because they work their fingers to the bone !

How do you make a skeleton laugh ?

Tickle his funny bone !

Who wrote the Japanese book of darning ?

Ho - Lin - Mee - Pants !

★

What's white and
hard and prickly ?

A skeleton that
needs a shave !

Joe - Why is an island like the letter T ?

Mum - They're both in the middle of water !

What gets wetter as you get drier ?

Your bath towel !

Waiter, waiter, there's a fly in my soup ?

**It's the rotten meat in there
that attracts them !**

★

I would tell you the
joke about the
fruit bowl

- but you would
go bananas !

And - I would tell you
the joke about
the prison

- but you're
never inmate !

Tarzan - Hello, operator, I want to speak to the King of the Jungle !

Operator - Sorry, the lion is busy !

★

We went round the world on holiday last year !

Where are you going this year ?

Oh, somewhere different !

How do you catch a vampire fish ?

With bloodworms !

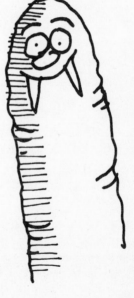

I've told you a million times not to exaggerate !

What's the difference between Bing Crosby and Walt Disney ?

Bing sings, but Walt Disney !

★

Little Miss Muffet
Sat on her tuffet
Eating her curds and whey
Along came a spider
and sat down beside her
so she squashed it !

Monster One - Should you eat chips
with your fingers ?

Monster Two - No, you eat chips with fish and
a salad with fingers !

Where do computers go to relax ?

To a disco !

What computer game did Robin Hood play ?

Super maid Mario !

What did the teacher ghost say to the talkative pupil ghost ?

Don't spook until you're spooken to !

Why is a bee like the police ?

They both have a sting in them !

What sort of car does an interior decorator drive ?

A Roller !

Did you hear about the man who was so mean that the moths in his wallet starved to death !

How do you make a horse box ?

Buy it a pair of boxing gloves and shorts !

What's the difference between a tube
and a stupid Dutchman ?

One is a hollow cylinder, the
other's a silly Hollander !

And I said to the man with the
long neck who sat in front of me
at the cinema...

...giraffe to sit there ?!

Jim - Does your watch tell the time ?

Joe - No, I have to look for myself !

Waiter, I can't eat this awful food -
fetch me the manager!

It's no good getting him, he didn't
want it either !

★

Joe -The dog keeps jumping up at my plate -
shall I give him a little of my dinner ?

Gran -Typical, he didn't want it when I put it in
his bowl this morning !

Sickly Smiles...

What do you call a bird that
falls under a lawn mower?

Shredded tweet!

After the monster had bitten off both my legs
the police refused to arrest him !

Why was that ?

They said he had no arm in him !

What's green and hairy and has 18 legs ?

I don't know !

**Neither do I, but it's just crawled
up into your shorts !**

Why did the chicken cross the road ?

I don't know !

**It was going for an eye test, which explains
why it got hit by a bus !**

What did the bus conductor say to the
monster with 3 heads, no arms and 1 leg ?

Hello, hello, hello you look armless, hop on !

Doctor - Stand in front
of the window and
stick out your tongue.

Patient -Are you going
to examine it ?

**Doctor -No, I just don't
like the man who lives in
the house opposite !**

What do you call a
deer with its eyes
poked out ?

No eye deer !

What do you call a dead deer with its
eyes poked out ?

Still no eye deer !

★

Those toffees were nice - but why were they furry ?

My mum sucked them up into the vacuum cleaner !

Why was the monster eating a horse in his bedroom at two in the morning ?

He was having a nighmare !

What's yellow, sticky and smells of bananas ?

Monkey sick !

What's the first thing a monster eats after he's had his teeth checked by the dentist ?

The dentist !

Where do you find monster snails ?

On the end of monsters' fingers !

Waiter - Why is there a frog in my soup ?

To catch the flies !

Waiter, why have you got your thumb in my soup ?

I have a boil on my thumb and the doctor said I have to keep it warm !

What's the best thing to do with a green monster ?

Wait until he's ripe or you'll get tummy ache after eating him !

Did you hear about the really stupid woodworm ?

It was found dead in a housebrick !

What is green and white and swings through the trees ?

Tarzan's handkerchief !

What is black and white and red at the bottom ?

A baby zebra with nappy rash !

What climbs up and down bellropes and is wrapped in a plastic bag ?

The lunchpack of Notre Dame !

What is black, floats on water and swears ?

Crude oil !

A fat man went into the doctors and asked if the doctor had anything to keep his belly in...

...here's a wheelbarrow !

311

Jim - If there are ten flies on a table and I kill one with a newspaper, how many will be left ?

Joe - Only the dead one !

What vegetable do you never want to see in a boat ?

A leek !

Who is that at the door ?

A man with a wooden leg.

Tell him to hop it !

Did you hear about the man with two wooden legs who caught fire ?

He burned down to the ground !

A little boy took a bucket into the living room and put it down in front of his elderly granny. He asked her to kick it - "'cos then my dad says we'll have plenty of money and I can have a new bike !"

Did you hear about the explorer
who escaped from the cannibals ?

It cost him an arm and a leg !

Doctor - You have four
minutes left to live !

Patient - What am I going to do ?

**Doctor - You could boil
me an egg ?!**

Your face is like a million dollars...

...all green and crinkly !

A man was sitting in the park with his baby in
his lap and he was clearly very angry. A passer
by asked him what was wrong.
The man replied "I have just been insulted in
that shop over there. They said my baby was
the ugliest child they had ever seen!"

**"That's terrible," replied the passer by,
"tell you what, you go in there and give
them a piece of your mind, I'll hold
your monkey for you !"**

Did you hear about the man who
stole a lorry load of prunes ?

He's been on the run for 6 months !

Mum, do steak pies have legs ?

No, dear, of course not !

Oh! Then grandad has just eaten the tortoise !

Why did the jockey take a bale of hay to bed ?

To feed his nightmares !

Why did the vampire have to go
and see his bank manager ?

**He had run up an overdraft on his
blood bank account !**

What is the difference between
a black cloud and someone who has just
had their toes run over ?

**One pours with rain
the other roars with pain !**

★

Waiter - why is there
a dead mouse in my soup ?

**You would be dead too
if you'd eaten any of it !**

★

Waiter, why are there
five pop singers in my soup ?

Well, you said you wanted it spicy !

★

Why should you always try to stay awake
when you are on a train ?

Because trains run over sleepers !

What did the doctor give the monster
for his liver ?

A kilo of onions !

What swings through trees backwards ?

Nazrat !

What did the zebra say on the
pedestrian crossing ?

**Now you see me
now you don't
now you see me
now you don't !**

Do you know him -
he's the hunchback
of Notre Dame ?

I don't know the
name - but his face
rings a bell !

This oatmeal tastes terrible - did you wash it before you cooked it ?

I certainly did, and here is the bar of oatmeal soap I washed it with !

★

A three legged monster went to the doctor to ask what he could do now that he had had his feet amputated.

You should take up a sport - try cricket - **they need three stumps !**

★

A monster was looking at his captive humans. He looked at one girl and said 'You look sweet!' The girl smiled, and the monster smiled back. 'OK,' said the monster, 'so that's pudding sorted, now for the main course!'

'Bring me a large Scotsman,' said the monster, **'I fancy eating a big mac !'**

How do you stop a skunk from smelling ?

Cut off it's nose !

What do you call a scruffy, unreliable and dishonest individual with no legs ?

A low down bum !

Doctor, doctor, I feel half dead !

Well, I will arrange for you to be buried from the waist down !

Doctor, doctor, I'm at death's door !

Don't worry, Mr. Blenkinsop, I'll soon pull you through !

Did you hear about the monster who told his girlfriend her face was as pretty as a flower...

...a cauliflower !

What Do You Call...?

What do you call a Scottish
cloak room attendant ?

Willie Angus McCoatup !

What do you call a man with a
calculator on his head ?

Adam !

What do you call a cat that
works in a chemists ?

Puss in Boots !

What is a rodent's favourite sport ?

Ka-rat-e !

What do you call someone with a pair of
shoes on their head ?

A sole singer !

What do call a man with six arms ?

Andy !

What do call a man with a bowl of custard on his head ?

Spotted Dick !

What do you call a man with a duck on his head ?

Quackers !

What do you call a small horse following someone ?

A pony tail !

What do you call a frog who can leave his car anywhere ?

A parking Kermit !

What do you call the college that a parrot goes to ?

A Polly-technic !

What do you call a man who can sing and drink lemonade at the same time ?

A pop singer !

What do you call a cat that is always having accidents ?

A catastrophe !

What do you call a machine for counting cows ?

A cowculator !

What do you call a robbery in Peking ?

A Chinese take-away !

What do you call the place where sick fairies go ?

The Elf Centre !

What do you call a doctor who works on the M1 ?

A by-pass specialist !

What do you call the man who
writes all Dracula's jokes ?

His crypt writer !

What do you
call the shark
who does
impersonations
of one of the
Beatles ?

Jaws Harrison !

What do you call work that fairies
have to do after school ?

Gnomework !

What do you call a streetlight where monsters
hang around waiting for victims ?

A ghoulpost !

What do you call the carpet cleaner that
vampires use ?

A victim cleaner !

What do you call it when your teacher is having
a baby ?

A miss-conception !

What do you call a spanner belonging
to a toad ?

A toad's tool !

What do you call the place where cats have
fashion shows ?

Catwalks !

What do you call a dead parrot ?

A polygon !

What do you call a Tibetan chicken ?

Himalaya !

What do you call someone who doesn't
use a hanky ?

Greensleeves !

What do you call a prisoner's pet budgie ?

A jailbird !

What do you call it when someone tries to
rob a bank with a bunch of flowers ?

Robbery with violets !

What do you call the largest mouse
in the world ?

Hippopotamouse !

What do you call it when you pick up the phone and send elephants charging in the opposite direction ?

A reverse-charge call !

What do you call a teddy bear's favourite drink ?

Ginger bear !

What do you call the skeleton who was once the Emperor of France ?

Napoleon Boney Parts !

What do you call a cat that works in a hospital ?

A first aid kit !

What do you call a cat that plays the drums ?

A drum kit !

What do you call a cat that makes models ?

A construction kit !

What do you call a snake that
grabs a cricketer ?

A bowler constrictor !

What do you call the last
man to abandon ship ?

Deaf !

What do you call the Elizabethan
explorer who could stop bicycles ?

Sir Francis Brake !

What do you call the explorer who was
caught and eaten by cannibals ?

Captain Cooked !

What do you call a man with a toilet
on his head ?

Lou !

*(Of course he might have two if he
was feeling flush !)*

What do you call twin brothers,
each with a drum on his head ?

Tom,Tom !

What do you call a cat in a panic ?

Cat flap !

What do you call the biggest ant in the World ?

An elephant !

What do you call a house where Martians live ?

A greenhouse !

What did the Martian say to the petrol pump ?

**Take your finger out of your ear
when I'm talking to you !**

What do you call a dog that likes
doing experiments ?

A Lab-rador !

What do you call the stuff your
milkman delivers if you live at the end of a
two mile cobbled street ?

Yogurt !

What do you call the dance where
all cakes are invited ?

Abundance !

What do you call it when two cows
munch grass side by side to keep warm ?

Double grazing !

What do you call a sheep dog when
it has eaten too much melon ?

Melancholy !

What do you call a highly dangerous cake ?

Atilla the bun !

What do you call the cake that was served
after the battle of the Little Big Horn ?

Custer's slices !

What do you call a cake you can use to
power your portable CD ?

Current cake !

What do you call a cake you can give to mice ?

Cheesecake !

What do you call a cake you eat in the bath ?

Sponge !

What do you call a dog that likes
wrapping presents ?

A boxer !

What do you call a madman who
has a wash then runs away ?

Nut, washes and bolts !

What do you call the Prime Minister's pet bunny ?

Blair rabbit !

What do you call a chimney built upside down ?

A well !

What do you call the most unhealthy bird ?

The Puffin !

What do you call the pliers you use in maths ?

Multipliers !

What do you call a 10p that can't go to the toilet ?

Coin-stipated !

What do you call stupid flowers that grow in a pond ?

Water sillies !

What do you call a sheep with fangs ?

A Lamb-pire !

What do you call a Shakespearian actor who eats garlic ?

Mac breath !

What do you call a the place where
aliens go to see films ?

Cine - Mars !

What do you call a skin complaint
that comes from London ?

Hackney !

What do you call a cat that only knows nine
stories and bores people to death with them ?

A cat-o-nine-tails !

What do you call a
machine for
counting snakes ?

An adder-ing machine !

What do you call someone who's been buried for 200 years ?

Peat !

What do you call the Gotham City superheroes after they have been run over by a steam roller ?

Flatman and Ribbon !

What do you call a doctor who operates without anaesthetic on her nieces and nephews ?

An agony aunt !

★

What do you call the young lady who lives in the coffin next to dracula's ?

The ghoul next door !

What do you call the woman who cleans out the school toilets ?

Lulu !

What do you call something with no legs that runs across the bathroom floor ?

Water !

What do you call the road where sword fights take place ?

A duel carriageway !

What sort of pet would a vampire own ?

A bloodhound !

★

Why couldn't the executioner decide what job he wanted to do ?

He kept chopping and changing !

What do you call out
when your toadstool
bag is almost full ?

There's not mushroom
in it now !

What do you call the
lectures about giblets
that monsters attend ?

Organ recitals !

What do you call the writer of books
about very old furniture ?

Anne Teak !

What do you call the children
of the Tsar of Russia ?

Tsar-dines !

What do you call the longest
night of the year ?

A fortnight !

What do you call a robbery when you know
you'll get away with it ?

A safe robbery !

What do you call a bicycle
that snarls at people ?

A vicious cycle !

What do you call the instrument
a skeleton plays ?

A trom - bone !

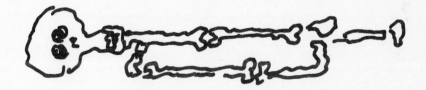

What do you call an MP with a
parrot on his shoulder ?

A polly-tician !

What do you call a
teddy that's been
buried in the garden ?

Plan - ted !

What do you call the flea on the moon ?

A lunar - tic !

What do you call a cat that you
can rest your head on ?

Cat - a - pillow !

What do you call the secret file on a dog ?

Con - fido - dential !

What do you call the place where a
cat does his cooking ?

The kit - chen !

Why was the snake charmer talking rubbish ?

He always talks cobras!

What do you call it when thousands of animals
rush to post letters ?

Stamp - ede !

What do you call the cross between a
cat and a butterfly ?

Kiterpillar !

How do you unload a ship full of snails ?

Open the escargot doors !

What do you call a man with a washing machine on his head on his head ?

Otto Matic !

What do you call a man with grass growing out of his head ?

Lorne !

What do you call spooky schoolbooks ?

Exorcise books !

What do you call the food that horses eat every day ?

Their stable diet !

What do you call six penguins in a supermarket ?

A packet of chocolate biscuits !

What do you call a vampire's favourite
hot breakfast cereal ?

Ready Neck !

What do you call a young dog
that eats flowers ?

A poppy !

When do monsters eat fried eyeballs ?

On fried - eyes !

What sort on creature ate my mum's sister ?

An aunt eater !

What do you call a flying dinosaur monster ?

Terror dactyl !

What do you call
a teacher
who turns
into a snake ?

Sir - pent !

How do you know when your teacher has
marked your homework with his wristwatch ?

There are ticks on the page !

What do you call a
very cheerful sweet ?

A Jolly Baby !

What do you call it when a witch feels
ill after travelling ?

Broom sick !

What sort of cake can you eat in the shower ?

A Bath bun !

What do you call a cake you eat in the bath ?

Sponge !

What do you call the skeleton of a snake ?

A rattler !

What is the result of smoking ?

Coffin !

What do you get if you get hit on
the head with an axe ?

A splitting headache !

What do you call the smelliest and hairiest
royal person in the World ?

King Pong !

What was the name of the man who
invented Italian radio ?

Macaroni !

What do you call the pliers you use in maths ?

Multipliers !

What do you a policeman with a
computer on his head ?

A PC !

Stupid Sports...

It was a terrible tragedy, one of the world's finest sprinters - died from pneumonia!

Look on the bright side - at least his nose kept running until the very end!

What job does Dracula have with the
Transylvanian cricket team ?

He looks after the bats !

Sporting Booklist...

How to win at sport

by

Vic Tree

Horse training

by

Jim Kana

The cricketers' quiz book

by

R.U. Stumped

How can you describe cricket in three words ?

Rain Stopped Play !

What do you call the cat playing football ?

Puss in boots !

My cousin has gold and silver medals in Karate, Cricket, Snooker, Horse Riding, High Jump, 200 Metres, Swimming, Marathon and Javelin !

Wow, he must be a super athlete !

No, he's a burglar actually !

Why has the groundsman
covered the grass in tar !?

Well - you told him to lay the
pitch out for tonight's match !

My Barry's in the Olympic
Archers team you know !

Goodness - he must be
a super shot ?

No, he's rubbish, but
he's heard every
episode of
the Archers!

Why are you hands covered in blood ?

Because I've just been giving a foot massage
to our Olympic team !

That's not usually a dangerous
thing to do is it ?

Only when they forget to take their spiked
running shoes off !

I knew Kevin was an underachiever when he had his Olympic gold medal bronze plated !

What do you call a spooky cricketer ?

A wicked keeper !

We'll never finish this bowling match !

What makes you say that ?

Well - every time I knock all the pins down, someone calls everyone out on strike !

What did it say on the snooker player's gravestone ?

Farewell to Jim, who has taken the long rest !

What was the name of that brilliant Russian billiards player ?

In off the red !

There was a time when he would get through
3 or 4 marathons a week - but he's not
touched one for months now !

Why is that ?

Well - they changed the name to Snickers !

Did you ever play for the
school football team, Blenkinsop ?

**I was left back, sir !
Left back in the changing rooms !**

You played a
magnificent innings
- let me oil
your bat !

**Why, I didn't
hear it squeaking !**

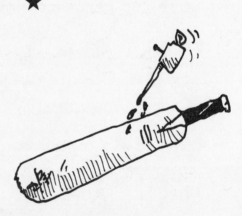

What game do elephants like playing
with people ?

Squash !

★

Alien Antics...

How do you know when a planet
gets engaged ?

You can see the ring !

How did the moon get a pat on the head ?

When the cow jumped over it !

Space Booklist...

Flying Saucers

by

Hugh Effo

They came from another planet

by

Marsha Nattack

How to build a rubber spaceship

by

Ben D Rocket

Where do spacemen go for a drink after work ?

A Mars Bar !

What do space monsters call humans ?

Breakfast, Lunch and Dinner !

How do you get a baby alien to sleep ?

Rocket !

What do aliens do at the disco ?

The Moonwalk !

Why do elephants paint themselves silver ?

So they can get a lift by grabbing on to the side of passing spaceships !

Well, I've never seen one do that !

Just shows what a good disguise it is !

What newspaper do aliens read ?

The Sun !

What do you call the vampire version of a favourite TV programme ?

Star Trek - the necks generation !

What do you call a spooky alien ?

Extra - terror - estrial !

Dad, in the future will spaceships run on time ?

Probably, what makes you ask that ?

Well, our teacher says they will still run on petrol !

How do students have to sit in robot school ?

Bolt upright !

ROBO
SKOOL

What is a robot's favourite film ?

Full Metal Jacket !

Where do newly-wed martians go after the service !

On a Honey - Earth !

★

Did you hear about the robot who went crazy, scrubbed his circuits clean and then ran off - it was in all the papers...

...Nut washers wires and bolts !

★

Did you hear about the cake that spotted a spaceship ?

It was a bun identified flying object !

★

Where do aliens go to listen to music ?

Nep-tune !

Hilarious Hobbies...

Ouch! Why do you keep standing
on my foot?

Someone told me you were a stamp collector!

Hobbies Bookshop...

Butterflies of the world

by

Chris Aliss

Bird Watching

by

Haydn Seekum

Drawing and Painting

by

Art N Design

Stamp Collecting

by

Phil Attlee

What do you mean you don't like pop music ?

**Well, would you listen to anything
your father liked !**

Where do you put
the lens cap when
you're taking
pictures ?

On Len's head !

How are you getting on with
your circuit training ?

**Well, it's made me a lot fitter, but we haven't
done any electronics at all yet !**

Why do you always paint rivers and
lakes in your pictures ?

Because I'm using water colours !

Why is it best to employ
an alien as a gardener ?

**Because they have
green fingers !**

How long have
you been interested
in keeping goats ?

Ever since I was a kid !

I didn't know your
daughter was interested
in computer games as well ?

**Yes, she's a microchip
off the old block !**

Why have you brought those cans of paint ?

Well, you said we were going trainspotting !

Hoy, you can't fish here,
this is a private lake !

**I'm not fishing, I'm teaching
my pet work to swim !**

Why are you putting
your wage packet
in with the bread mixture ?

**I'm hoping it will
give me a raise in pay !**

★

That's amazing - whenever
you ring a bell your dog runs
into the corner and sits down ?!

That's because he's a boxer !

★

These buns you've
cooked taste of
soap !

**That's because
they're Bath buns !**

Why did you give up tap dancing then ?

I kept falling into the sink !

Can you telephone
from a submarine ?

**Of course - a phone
won't work
underwater !**

I think I'll take up jogging !

**Well you had better start with your memory -
because you forgot my birthday again !**

What do electronics enthusiasts
have on their sarnies ?

Radio Ham !

Final Fling...

Whose daddy was a mummy ?

Tutankhamen !

Joe - Last night I opened the door
in my pyjamas !

Jim - Why on earth have you got a door in
your pyjamas ?

What do you call a bird drinking two drinks
at once ?

Toucan !

Did you hear about the monster who ate
a settee and two chairs for lunch ?

He had a three piece suite tooth !

Mum, can you help me with my maths homework,
I'm trying to find the lowest common
denominator ?

Crickey, they were trying to find that
when I was at school !

Why did the fly fly ?

Because the spider spied her !

What do you get if you cross
a pig with a dinosaur ?

Jurassic Pork !

When the monster had finished his tea he
asked his mum if he could leave the table.

**She said yes he could, as long as
he had eaten the chairs !**

Did you hear about the stupid burglar
who threw two bricks through the
jewellers window...

**...Because someone told him they had
double glazing !**

Which snake tells tales ?

The grass snake !

What do you call an environmentally friendly,
noiseless, biodegradable food mixer that uses
no electricity ?

A wooden spoon !

How do you stop a mouse from squeaking ?

Oil it !

Which two kings were good at fractions ?

Richard the third and Henry the eighth !

Who was the first man on the moon ?

A spaceman !

What lies under your bed at night with its
tongue hanging out ?

Your shoe !

Why was the cat lying on the toast rack ?

It was a marmalade cat !

What would happen to a penguin
in the desert ?

The chocolate would melt !

Have you heard about the boy who kept
a pencil in his bedroom...

**...so he could draw the curtains
every morning !**

*Little Miss Muffet
sat on a tuffet,
eating tandoori and rice.
A monster from Bury
ate Miss Muffet and curry,
and said 'by golly that was nice !'*

Teacher - Name three birds that can't fly ?

***Pupil* - An ostrich and two dead sparrows !**

Waiter, why is this chop
so tough?

It's a Karate chop, sir!

KEEEAAA!!!

★

Joe -Which is the best side to have
the handle of a teacup on?

Jim - The outside!

★

I would tell you the
joke about quicksand...

...but it might take a
while to sink in!

★

I wish you wouldn't cheat
when we play cards!

How do you know I'm cheating?

Because you're not playing
the hand I dealt you!

What do you do with a red monster ?

Take it back to the library and
get another one to read !

What is a good
parting gift ?

A comb !

What did the Pink Panther say when he
stood on an ant ?

Dead Ant, Dead Ant,
Dead Ant Dead Ant Dead Ant
Dead Ant Dead Ant...

How do ducks play tennis ?

They use a tennis quack-it !

Why did the cannibal go to the wedding ?

**Because he heard they were going
to toast the bride and groom !**

★

Hostess - Does this aeroplane travel
faster than the speed of sound

No Madam !

Good, because my husband and I want to talk !

★

What is the longest night ?

A fortnight !

★

Booklist...

The complete gardener

by

Rosa Cabbage

How to combat stiffness

by

Arthur Ritus

The Sandwich Makers Book

by

Roland Butter

The Titanic Story

by

I.C. Water

What does a music teacher take to the
supermarket ?

A Chopin Liszt !

What did the tie say to the hat ?

You go on ahead and I'll hang around here !

Operator, can you put me
through to the zoo ?

Sorry, the lion is engaged !

What can you tell me about the Dead Sea ?

Crikey, I didn't even know it was sick !

How do you flatten a spook ?

Use a spirit level !

What do you call a homeless snail ?

A slug !

**Little Miss Muffet
sat on a tuffet,
eating a piece of cheese.
Along came a mouse
the size of a house,
now little Miss Muffet's deceased !**

Teacher - I wish you would pay
a little attention Blenkinsop !

Pupil - I'm paying as little as I can !

Why were you breaking the speed limit ?

**I was trying to get home before
my petrol ran out !**

Where were all the Kings
and Queens of France
crowned ?

On the head !

What is the best time to pick apples ?

When the farmer is away on holiday !

How does a woman know when she has fallen in love with a cricket player?

She is completely bowled over!

Spell a hungry bee in three letters!

M T B!

Why did the sprinter run across everyone sitting in the park?

Because his trainer told him to run over twenty laps!

How do you make a cat happy?

Send it to the Canary Isles!

What sort of pens do cry babies use?

Bawl points

What do you call a a chimney
built upside down ?

A well !

Who is Postman Pat's favourite actor ?

Terence Stamp !

Why do oysters never share their sweets ?

Because they are shell fish !

What do you call a prisoner's budgie ?

A jail bird !

When are you allowed to take toffee to school ?

On a chews day !

History teacher -
Can anyone tell me what a forum is ?

Blenkinsop -
A two-um plus a two-um sir ?!

Pupil - What is this ?

Dinner attendant - It's bean soup !

Pupil - Maybe, but what is it NOW !

Why are teachers welcome in snooker halls ?

Because they always bring their own chalk !

Where do teachers get all their information ?

From Fact - ories !

Why do doctors hate teachers when they come
to see them ?

Because they never give them enough
time to do the examination !

Knock Knock...
Who's there ?
Scot...
Scot who ?
Scot nothing to do with you !

Knock Knock...
Who's there ?
Cher...
Cher who ?
Cher this orange with me - it's too big
for me to eat on my own!

Knock Knock...
Who's there ?
Bob...
Bob who ?
**Bob down and I'll pass your letters
through the catflap !**

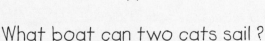

What boat can two cats sail ?

A catamaran !

What goes moo, moo, splash !?

A cow falling into the sea !

Why was the baby goat a crazy mixed up kid ?

Because he fell into the spin dryer !

What does a
mouse say when
you take his
photograph ?

CHEESE !

**Boyfriend / Girlfriend
speak...**

You have the body of a
Greek god...
really means...

**...you look like you're
hiding a statue
under your jumper !**

You're a very interesting person...*really means...*

...I wish you wouldn't talk so much !

I'd love you to come for tea...*really means...*

**...Anything is better than being seen out on
the street with you !**

My parents think you're great...really means...

...They think someone as weird as you
will put me off boys/girls for
the next 10 years !

★

What do monsters fasten their
suitcases to the car roof-rack with ?

Franken - twine !

What does Dracula tow
behind his car
on holiday ?

A Caravanpire !

Why do monsters not mind being
eaten by kindly ghosts ?

Because they know they
will always be in good spirits !

Who brings Christmas presents
to werewolves ?

Santa Claws !

Well, Mr. Blenkinsop, your cough sounds much
better this morning !

**So it should, doctor, I've been up
all night practising !**

★

Doctor, doctor, I think I'm a dog !

Well, take a seat and I'll have
a look at you !

I can't - I'm not allowed on the furniture !

Doctor, doctor, my wife thinks
I'm a hypochondriac !

Why haven't you been to see me before about
this ?

I've been too ill !

★

Doctor, doctor, I
think I will have to
give up jogging !

Why ?

**Because whenever I
stop my nose
keeps running !**

★

What do you get if you cross a
frog and a fizzy drink ?

Croaka - cola !

★

What game do you get if you cross a
skunk and a cartoon penguin ?

Pingu - pong !

What do you get if you cross a fruit and a woman who needs help ?

A damson in distress !

What do you get if you train a reindeer to be a hairdresser ?

Styling Mousse !

Wow, it's hot in this stadium, I'm boiling !

Well, come and stand next to me - I'm a fan !

Why are you putting that apple
in the rowing boat ?

You told me to put the cox in !?

★

"One hundred and eighty !"

I'm new to darts - is that a good score ?

Score ? - That's his waist measurement !!

What is a vampire's favourite sport ?

Point to point ?

Who serves the meals on a spooky aeroplane ?

The Air Ghostess !

What do you call a German barber ?

Herr Dresser !

Did you hear about the man who went
to the doctor and told him he
thought he was a piano ?

The doctor gave him a note !

What do you get if you cross a pig
with a hedgehog ?

A porkupine !

Why do teddy bears never hear what you say ?

Because they have cloth ears !

What sort of takeaway food
do aliens like best ?

Nuclear Fission Chips !

What sort of fish flies a spaceship ?

A Pilot Whale !

Have you heard about the
inter-galactic magicians club -

- called the flying sorcerers !

Which cartoon character is really a robot ?

Tin - Tin !

What is the name of the computerised
policeman ?

PC PC !

Our games teacher once tried to swim across the English channel !

Did he do it ?

No - He got halfway across and had to turn back because he was so tired !

Music teacher - Why are you standing on that chair ?

Pupil - So I can reach the high notes !

Doctor, doctor, I'm suffering from paranoia !

Well, I would be too, if so many people were out to get me !

Doctor, doctor, I feel like a bird !

Well, you've come to the right place for tweetment !

What do you call a noble Egyptian mummy ?

Sir Cophagus !

★

What do you call a
wobbly book full
of telephone numbers ?

A jellyphone directory !